LEAD
— WITH —
COURAGE

Unleash the Lion in You

ARTHUR E. PUOTINEN

BALBOA
PRESS

A DIVISION OF HAY HOUSE

Balboa Press books may be ordered through booksellers or by contacting:

Balboa Press
A Division of Hay House
1663 Liberty Drive
Bloomington, IN 47403
www.balboapress.com
1 (877) 407-4847

Because of the dynamic nature of the Internet, any web addresses or
links contained in this book may have changed since publication and
may no longer be valid. The views expressed in this work are solely those
of the author and do not necessarily reflect the views of the publisher,
and the publisher hereby disclaims any responsibility for them.

The author of this book does not dispense medical advice or prescribe the use
of any technique as a form of treatment for physical, emotional, or medical
problems without the advice of a physician, either directly or indirectly. The
intent of the author is only to offer information of a general nature to help
you in your quest for emotional and spiritual well-being. In the event you use
any of the information in this book for yourself, which is your constitutional
right, the author and the publisher assume no responsibility for your actions.

Any people depicted in stock imagery provided by Thinkstock are models,
and such images are being used for illustrative purposes only.
Certain stock imagery © Thinkstock.

Print information available on the last page.

ISBN: 978-1-5043-4189-9 (sc)
ISBN: 978-1-5043-4188-2 (e)

Library of Congress Control Number: 2015915985

Balboa Press rev. date: 10/26/2015

Contents

Endorsements

Art and I go back a long way. We first became friends in the 1970s when he was dean of the faculty and I was dean of students at Suomi College in Hancock, Michigan. The athletic teams at Suomi were known as the Lions. Male, female, spectator—all were known as Lions. And Art Puotinen was the most lionhearted of us all, through good times and tough times in his fierce, unflinching dedication to the college, his family, his calling, and his faith. He still is! Anyone seeking direction, counsel, assurance, and support, no matter where they are at in their life journey, can benefit from reading Art's book.

Rev. Dave Strang

Lead with Courage is grounded in the life experiences of an experienced leader who has led in a variety of faith-based and nonprofit settings. Art's personal story is woven in ways to share leadership lessons with the reader. Part memoir and part leadership guide, readers will enjoy seeing the lessons of leadership unfold in the pages of this book.

Dave Daubert, consultant and pastor, Day 8 Strategies

To
Judy Cathleen Puotinen,
teacher, artist, mother/grandmother, presidential spouse;

Anne, Marjetta, and Sara Puotinen,
dear daughters in life's journey; and

Carol Schaley Puotinen,
beloved new life partner.

Foreword

It is a joy to introduce you to one of my coaching students, Arthur Puotinen. He has read several of my books, has attended my presentations in Canada and the United States, and now has completed a major homework task. His new book, *Lead with Courage: Unleash the Lion in You*, results from my 10-10-10™ program, which offers persons the opportunity to write their own book of ten chapters in ten hours of their own time and to hold their published book in their hands in ten weeks. He chose to write fifteen chapters, completing this inspiring and informative memoir with personal stories and numerous strategies to help others in their life journey.

Puotinen's new book documents his expertise and leadership experiences in the fields of business, education, and spiritual life. His primary focus is on individuals and organizations that are learning and growing to reach for achievement and significance. He believes that courage is essential to survive and thrive in life and leadership. This attribute is evident in lions in their natural setting and in humans in personal and social settings. Courage is especially crucial in overcoming various challenges and crises that occur in various stages of life.

Examples of courage in the book are portrayed in such formative experiences as family life and heritage; school and college experiences;

courtship and marriage; writing and public speaking; leading groups and organizations; fundraising for projects, financial crises, and recovery; facing cancer; and retirement.

As a further resource, Art and Carol Puotinen have created ACLION Investments LLC to provide assistance with real estate transactions, organizational planning and funding, and information exchange.

Raymond Aaron, *New York Times* best-selling author

Preface

There is a leader in you and a leader in me. Leadership is a process in which good people work together to make good things happen. You have talents and strengths to bring to groups, teams, and organizations. In working together, we discover our complementary talents for leadership. Together we can do more.

My career vision is to preach, teach, and lead. My preaching experience included being a parish pastor in four congregations and leading worship one to two Sundays a month in local churches while being a college academic dean and president. My teaching experience ranged from a full-time appointment at Central Michigan University to one or two courses a semester while serving as a college dean and other short-term teaching experiences in church and community settings. Leadership occurred in small groups, local institutions, and national organizations that overcame difficulties and experienced growth. Preaching, teaching, and leading are my positions to play, and I thank my many mentors, colleagues, family members, and friends that taught and encouraged me in my career fields.

I have written this book for several reasons. As a memoir for my family, it preserves some elements of our heritage. As a legacy of lessons learned in leadership experiences in ministry, educational administration, and business, it offers information and insights on opportunities to serve, challenges to face, and blessings to receive.

As a self-help book, it offers leaders at various levels practical, how-to examples and thought-provoking questions for personal reflection and discussion. As a spiritual book, it reveals that faith and courage are gifts from God to help us face crises, resolve conflicts, and enjoy our lives and work.

My mentor at the University of Chicago Divinity School, Dr. Martin E. Marty, offered many constructive suggestions in writing this book. Lutheran pastor Dr. Dave Daubert helped me at various stages. And my close friend Rev. Dave Strang and his wife, Donna, supported me in my journey.

To my family, friends, colleagues, and others that accompanied me on my pilgrimage of faith, thank you for your encouragement and help. To God be the glory.

INTRODUCTION

The Lion in You

You have a birthright to lead and to claim your identity, purpose, and potential. This self-discovery will shape your future. I heard Peter Setzer of Hickory, North Carolina, tell the following story:

> Once upon a time, a little lion became lost from his parents. He was discovered by a flock of sheep. They taught him how to *baaah* because that's what everybody in the flock did. They taught him how to munch on *graaass* that tasted lousy, but that's what everybody in the flock did.
>
> One day, the little lion was out in the field, munching on some grass. Suddenly he heard footsteps and turned around. Standing there was a large lion with a magnificent mane. He let loose with a mighty *roaaar* and then said to the little lion, "What are you doing here?"
>
> The little lion was sheepish and said hesitantly, "I'm munching on *graaass.*"
>
> The big lion stood tall and said, "Follow me!"

The big lion and little lion walked for a while together until they came to a small pool. Then the big lion told him, "Now look into the water."

Obediently the little lion gazed into the water and saw his own likeness for the first time. Then he turned to the big lion and exclaimed, "Hey, I look just like you!"

The older lion roared, "Now you know *who* and *whose* you are. Come along, follow me, and show me what you can be and do."

This story resonates with a truth: we need mentors to give us a wake-up call—to help affirm our identities and potential, our talents and possibilities. Feeling unfulfilled where we are, unaware of our opportunities, or unsure of what to do, we look for new ideas and prospects. Problems at work or school, health concerns, work failures, strained relationships, the loss of loved ones, and other issues sometimes confront us. These challenges awaken the lion in us to come forth and face these situations with courage.

A poet writes, "A lion paces in every human heart. What quickens yours? What makes your lion roar?" The attributes a lion exemplifies are strength, courage, power, royalty, dignity, authority, dominion, justice, wisdom, and ferocity.[1] A lion is part of a pride, or group, where survival skills are learned and practiced. The processes of leadership are a way of life for the young and older lions that inhabit jungles and other locales. Naturally abundant with many resources, such settings are both beautiful and dangerous. Lions, like humans, must overcome fear and hesitancy to respond to challenges and crises.

Fear creeps in when dangers appear. Perhaps you don't know what to do when fears keep you from taking decisive action. During a financial crisis facing one of the colleges I worked at, it helped me to write down all my fears for our school, our constituents, my family, and me. It was the first time I had ever written such a list, and I told my wife, "Sometimes you need to look the tiger in the teeth and count every tooth."

This act of describing my fears led me to remember President Franklin Delano Roosevelt, who rallied a nation with these words: "The only thing we have to fear is fear itself." Calming and overcoming my fears led me to two of my favorite Bible passages by the Apostle Paul: "I can do all things through Christ who strengthens me" (Philippians 4:13) and "the power by which God raised Jesus from the dead is alive and at work in you" (Romans 8:11). Or you may prefer these words of Mark Twain: "Courage is resilience to fear, mastery of fear, not absence of fear."

When fear, apprehension, and worry weigh down your spirit, it's time to unleash the courageous lion in you and become the person you are destined to be. Like a lion,

- hold your head high, even in times of conflict, and conduct yourself with dignity;
- stand tall, and remember your birthright of power;
- show your authority—not in a dominating way but by leading others with a caring heart;
- protect and defend something or someone that is dear to your heart; and
- be courageous and have faith.

In this book about becoming a better leader, I recall lessons learned, mistakes made, losses endured, and achievements earned. Sharing these story with you is therapeutic, and it's a heartfelt thank-you to and affectionate remembrance of the many mentors, loved ones, and friends that have shaped my life. Many will be introduced to you in my story. They helped to unleash the courageous lion in me with their love, encouragement, vision, and discipline.

Each of the fifteen chapters has three parts:

- how lions live and survive in their natural habitat
- how leaders face challenges and crises and learn from their shortcomings and success
- how leadership suggestions and lessons may be used in your own life and work

Each chapter also includes several self-reflection topics for you to consider. Take a few moments to share your thoughts in a journal or in a conversation with a friend, as if you were conversing with me. I hope you enjoy this feature of the book and find it useful.

Lead with Courage narrates personal leadership experiences from my childhood up to my retirement. The chapters relate the importance of courage in formative experiences:

- family life
- school and college studies
- courtship and marriage
- vision for life and vocation
- writing and public speaking
- top leadership responsibilities
- financial crises and recovery
- overcoming grief when loved ones die
- active retirement

CHAPTER 1

Discover Your Family Heritage

Lion cubs grow up in a lion family, better known as a pride. Raising cubs is a collective task in which females feed, protect, and nurture their own cubs as well as other young ones in the pride. Male lions spend a lot of time with the pride when the cubs are little, watching them play and tolerating their behavior with less patience than the lionesses do. Lions look and listen when they hunt together, and young lions learn from their elders.[2]

In the human situation, we learn a great deal through our family experiences. Today families are described as traditional, extended, blended, and in other ways. Your family pride includes the ideals you hold, the habits you cherish, and the love you share. Your expression of your family values, successes, and struggles affirm your family pride and the perspectives that shape the emerging leader in you.

You Value Your Family Leaders

Share an example of how your parents, grandparents, or other family members demonstrated leadership.

Getting started with stories of the older lions in your family may lead you to trace your family tree, examine family pictures and records, and even write a short story or a book! It happened to me, and following is a bit of the Puotinen family heritage.

I lived with my paternal grandparents and parents on our family farm of eighty acres in Upper Michigan. The back forty had abundant fields and forests, and the Hemlock River ran through them. My grandpa and dad took me to the river to fish for trout. Standing on the bank, holding a fishing pole, and waiting for the fish to bite on the earthworms on a line gives a young kid great memories to treasure. Catching a twelve-inch rainbow trout and holding it was one of the most memorable for me.

Those bigger lions took me, the little lion, to my pool of discovery. Imagine this scene: The Hemlock River current came rapidly from upstream, then moved in waves over the rocks before me, and finally moved downstream around the bend toward the larger Paint River several miles away. In my daydreams at the river's edge, I looked at and listened to the water and felt the current of my own spirit. These questions came to mind: Where did the river come from? Why are the rapids before me turbulent? Where is the river going; what is its destination? My questions turned to these thoughts: Where did I come from? What should I do now in my life? What will my future be when I leave the river and the farm?

Perhaps you have a river story or similar experience from your childhood or a different place that prompted you to ask those three questions. Maybe your story has a mentor, such as a parent or teacher, that brought you to the river of life to search for your identity and purpose.

One of my earliest memories was hearing my grandparents tell their stories of their life and adventures together. My paternal grandparents were Elias Puotinen (born March 25, 1869) and Johanna Bjorbacka (born February 2, 1876). They resided not far from each other in Evijarvi, Finland, in the northern lake country. Elias and Johanna were part of the Finnish Lutheran church, which was undergoing a spiritual awakening.

Nurtured in the Christian faith and a strong work ethic, they moved separately to the Upper Peninsula of Michigan. Elias arrived in Crystal Falls on October 28, 1886, and Johanna came six years later on August 9, 1892. Like many immigrants past and present, they came to the United States in search of a new life. They left behind family members and friends in Finland, traveled the Atlantic Ocean onboard a ship, arrived at Ellis Island in New York, and then took a train to Michigan. Their sponsor in Crystal Falls was an immigrant Finn named Emil Hurja, who also helped other Finns resettle in Michigan.

Millions of families today have similar stories in which their forebears left the familiar surroundings of their homeland and migrated to a new country, seeking a new life. Each family has its own story of that eventful passage of an earlier generation. Why did these folks uproot themselves and head out for a new world and way of life? What were their hopes and dreams? Where did they go, find work, and settle in? How did they adjust, survive, and even thrive in their new environment?

You Discover Three Generations

Take time to discover the names of your parents and grandparents, their ethnic backgrounds, and their employment opportunities.

A Finnish immigrant once told me this:

> My young wife and I decided to move to Michigan because we heard there were jobs in the mines and forests. Some other Finns from our village in Finland had moved there earlier. They wrote and encouraged us to come because opportunities for jobs, homes, and raising a family were good. So we decided to pack up and go to the Copper Country of Michigan.
>
> The trip was long. We went by ship to New York and then by train to Chicago and northward to the Upper Peninsula of Michigan until we arrived at Hancock, in the heart of the copper mining area. I remember when we got off the train and walked up the rocky street from the depot. There was no gold on the street, just mounds of slag rock from the mines on either side. My wife saw this strange new setting and began to sob. She remembered the farming community and families we left behind in Finland.
>
> As we continued walking, she stubbed her toe on something. It was a paper bag with a blessing in it. I opened the bag and pulled out a loaf of freshly baked bread. I handed it to her, put my arm around her, and said, "See, the Lord is already providing for us in this wilderness."

The story of my family is about discovering opportunities, receiving blessings, and raising a family. After arriving and adjusting to living and working conditions in a "free country," Elias and Johanna were married and began a new life together after acquiring eighty acres of land twelve miles north of Crystal Falls and two miles out of Amasa, Michigan. Amasa received its name from the iron-mining Mather family that earlier named their son Amasa Mather. Immigrant Finns and other ethnic groups moved into the area to make their living in logging, iron mining, and farming. Five churches and five taverns in Amasa became gathering places for local residents and newcomers. A railroad station welcomed occasional visitors and transported material goods to and from the area to Houghton County in the north and to Chicago to the south.

Elias and Johanna started farming by clearing the front forty acres of trees and rocks with help from neighbors. Earning their blessing of daily bread became an immediate quest. First they erected a Finnish sauna (a two-room steam bath) from logs and rocks in a clearing. Then they built a two-story, four-bedroom farmhouse with help from neighbors. It eventually became home to twelve sons and daughters in this birth order: Emil, Aino, Eino, Ilma, Onni, Jenny, Heino, Kaleva, Toivo, Eva, Viljo, and Ellen.

Grandpa Eli, the sons, and their neighbors erected a barn for the cows on the first floor, hay storage on the second floor, and a refrigerated milk storage area. Several family members milked their Guernsey cows by hand twice a day. The Puotinens used whole milk at home for drinking, cheese, and yogurt. They also sold milk to wholesalers in Crystal Falls. They grew and harvested oats and barley grain. They planted, cultivated, and picked potatoes for home and commercial use.

The back forty of the farm was mainly woods with an occasional small field after stumps were cleared. The Hemlock River bordered one side of the property, and it became a favorite site for trout fishing and swimming. Deer and ruffed grouse roamed in the woods; so did hunters in October and November.

My grandparents were enterprising role models, being both entrepreneurs and founders of several organizations. Johanna was a quiet yet strong woman who cared for her children and the cows with diligence and patience. Elias ran the farm and broadened his reach into the community. He platted sections of local lands, sold farm implements and fire insurance, started a logging operation, and gained a local reputation for his resourcefulness. My grandparents were among the founders of Bethany Lutheran Church in Amasa, the local Amasa consumer cooperative store, and the Flower in the Dale Temperance Society.

Elias and Johanna valued education and industrious work, and several of their children received a college-level education and had careers away from Upper Michigan. My parents, Kaleva and Ines, raised me as their only child and provided home care for Elias and Johanna until they passed in their eighties. Finnish was my first language at home, and English became my dominant tongue while attending public school in Crystal Falls. My teachers and classmates helped me discover the larger world.

My other maternal grandparent, Elona Hedvig Maki (born in 1886), was from Kauhajoki, Finland, and migrated to the Crystal Falls in 1900. Her husband, Samuel Maki, passed in 1936. They raised a family of seven children in a farming community midway between Amasa and Crystal Falls. Their children included John and Martha from a previous marriage and their own children: Elona, Ines, Ilmi, Tynie, Waino, and Arne. Mother Elona was a remarkable woman who practiced folk medicine and had prophetic insight. She was a skilled midwife and devoted mother while managing a small farm.

You Receive Wisdom

Take a moment to remember and note one or more bits of wisdom you received from an older member of your family.

My paternal and maternal grandparents gave me a gift for storytelling and for gathering the stories of others. Their example and heritage also led me to visit Finland and their hometown of Evijarvi, where the Puotinen life journey began. Meeting family members there in 1992 and 2002 confirmed the reasons for my family pride. In the first visit, my wife, Judy, and I were a Rotary International Exchange couple, so we met with Rotarians living and working in various communities in Finland. Everywhere we went, we asked them about their economic good times and hard times, about getting along with their Russian neighbors, and about what they did for a good time.

In Evijarvi, we enjoyed a noon meal with Puotinen family members. The gathering included a young lad of ten years who resembled me at that age. Overall, the visit gave me a greater sense of wholeness, confidence, and determination to succeed in my life's vocation.

Telling the story of your family and their times may even lead to writing a book. My MA and PhD graduate studies at the University of Chicago Divinity School prepared me for scholarly research and a career in higher education. Many gifted teachers opened different fields of knowledge to me, and my graduate school mentor, Dr. Martin E. Marty, encouraged and guided me in my doctoral dissertation preparation. He encouraged me to go deeper into my family heritage and the Progressive Era and to discover a story that needed to be told as part of the American experience.

You Find Family Facts

Interview a family member or friend who knows your grandparents, and write down interesting facts about them.

My first book, *Finnish Radicals and Religion in Midwestern Mining Towns, 1865–1914,* chronicles the Finnish immigrant experience in the copper and iron mining regions of Michigan and Minnesota. My research describes the historical conditions in Finland that prompted many Finns to migrate to the United States during this time period. The immigrants responded to numerous challenges upon their arrival in their new surroundings. Arno Press published this thesis as part of their Scandinavians in America series in 1983. More than an academic exercise this book became my earnest endeavor to gain greater knowledge of my ethnic and spiritual heritage, regional environment, and major economic and social issues.

My dissertation research began in earnest in the fall of 1970. The English and Finnish language sources were mainly in Upper Michigan and Minnesota. I found copper and iron mining research materials at Michigan Technological University in Houghton near Lake Superior and at the Minnesota State History Library in Saint Paul. And I found Finnish immigrant history records in Finnish and English in the Finnish American Historical Archives at Suomi College in Hancock, Michigan.

It was a journey born with hope and little money. Before moving to Hancock, I had been serving as pastor of Trinity Lutheran Church on Wilson Avenue in Chicago while commuting to the University of Chicago Divinity School for graduate study. There I received my master's in church history in 1969, took my other qualifying PhD exams, and did coursework. The dissertation was my next major step, and the move to the northland was a scholarly necessity and a journey of faith.

My wife, Judy, gave birth in Chicago to our daughter Marjetta (whom we call Marji) in August of 1970, joining her three-year old sister, Anne. We headed to the Upper Peninsula a month later. We rented a small Suomi College–owned house in Hancock. Judy cared for our girls as I did archival research on Finnish migration to Michigan in the Finnish American Historical Archives and on regional economic developments at Michigan Technological University in Houghton.

I generated some funds by occasionally preaching on Sundays at nearby churches and assisted Suomi College President Ralph Jalkanen in editing and publishing his book *Faith of the Finns*. I also received encouragement and support from my parents, who lived ninety miles away near Amasa on the Puotinen family farm, and from Judy's parents, John and Orliss Kapoun. They lived in West Saint Paul and hosted us during family visits and my research in the Minnesota State History Library.

My research and writing on the Finnish American experience in Michigan and Minnesota eventually produced one book, five chapters in other books, and other publications.[3] My primary theme in these works was Finnish immigrant life, economic justice, and social conflict. A decisive chapter in *Finnish Radicals and Religion in Midwestern Mining Towns, 1865–1914* recalls the Copper Country Strike of 1913, which involved labor and management struggles at a time when mining had been booming in Michigan's Upper Peninsula. Investors received substantial profit from the underground copper while employing immigrant Finns and other nationalities.

The Western Federation of Miners, seeking to organize the miners for better wages and benefits, led a strike of a multiethnic labor force on the Fourth of July weekend of 1913. Confrontations occurred between strikers and company representatives at various mines and nearby towns. The Michigan governor sent the state national guard to the area to maintain law and order. Companies hired their own deputies to manage mining-site activities. Several violent incidents occurred, and local communities were divided into those who favored or opposed the strike. My book focused on how the immigrant Finns became involved in the conflict and how they coped afterward.

The turning point in the strike occurred at the tragic Italian Hall disaster in Calumet on Christmas Eve 1913. Copper miner families gathered to celebrate in the upstairs community room when someone yelled, "Fire!" Seventy-three men, women, and children were crushed to death as they tried to exit down a stairway through the double exit doors downstairs. The press of the crowd barred any attempts to open the doors to freedom. I was moved to tears when viewing pictures of some of the victims placed side by side on tables. (See Chapter 7 in *Finnish Radicals*, pp. 242-288 for a fuller account of the 1913 Copper Strike.)

In the 1970s, I visited the upstairs floor of the Italian Hall with a retired miner named Al Harvey, who had witnessed the 1913 tragedy. Folding chairs were still strewn around the place, like it was a day or two after the tragedy. Radio-broadcasted interviews of survivors and witnesses of the Christmas Eve event awakened my resolve to tell the story of the strike. Conflict became the dominant motif of my book and eventually led me to other conflict situations that tested my abilities as a leader.

You Discover Truth

Take a moment to note here your discovery of an important fact or story that moved you to tell others in writing or speaking.

I completed my book *Finnish Radicals and Religion in Midwestern Mining Towns* after obtaining a teaching position for three years as assistant professor of Religious Studies at Central Michigan University. In 1974, President Jalkanen of Suomi College appointed me to be its academic dean, a position that involved teaching, administration, and grant writing.

Earlier in 1972, President Jalkanen and I collaborated on a project grant proposal entitled "Finnish Folklore and Social Change in the Great Lakes Mining Region" from the National Endowment for the Humanities. They funded it for five years. (My research design for the project [see footnote 3] identified the materials to be gathered.) That summer, we assembled a group of interviewers to gather stories from residents in Michigan and Minnesota. Using a flexible interview format we tape-recorded recollections from men and women in various locales about the good times and hard times as economic and social changes occurred in the mining regions. The interviews were an in-depth refinement of the three questions I'd had by the Hemlock River as a youth: Where did you and your family come from? What are the struggles and successes you have experienced in this place? What do you envision for the future for your family and this region?

The Finnish American Historical Archives in Hancock summarized the scope of the "Finnish Folklore and Social Change in the Great Lakes Mining Region Oral History Project 1972–1978":

A large collection of oral histories from the Copper Country (in the Upper Peninsula of Michigan) and northeastern Minnesota were recorded in the 1970s by staff and students of Suomi College, now Finlandia University. Rev. Dr. Arthur Puotinen led the project and received a grant from the United States National Endowment for the Humanities. While there are many interviews with Finnish Americans from the Great Lakes Region, the scope of the project also included people from other communities and ethnic groups, and includes clergy, lawmen, doctors, and business leaders such as William Parsons Todd of the Quincy Mining Company. There are approximately 250 hours of transcribed interviews and about 150 hours of non-transcribed interviews. The tapes and transcripts are located at Finlandia University's Finnish American Historical Archive and Museum in Hancock, Michigan.[4]

In 2010, the Finnish American Historical Archive and Museum received a generous grant from the Keweenaw National Historic

Park Advisory Commission to digitize the extensive Finnish Folklore and Social Change in the Great Lakes Mining Region Oral History collection.

Complete interviews are available to visiting researchers at the Finnish American Historical Archives in Hancock, as are online excerpts from various interviews.

Finnish Radicals and Religion in Midwestern Mining Towns, 1865—1914 is out of print, with only a few copies on Amazon now and then. The creation of the Suomi College Oral History Project, however, is an example of how a founding vision, funding support, and a cadre of interviewers and interviewees can capture bits of community history and memories, a sponsoring institution (Finlandia University), and technological preservation. It is a legacy gift to those interested in discovering their heritage and writing their own blog, article, or book.

You Offer Your Legacy to Others

Take a moment to express how you wish to be remembered after you leave a place of residence, a workplace, or a relationship.

You have your story to share with others. You may have family leaders and family pride to inspire and inform you. Perhaps you have friends, mentors and/or others that shape your story. Your discovery will be a journey of listening and learning in a variety of ways. Pictures, audio and video sources, written records, travel to important locales, and conversations with interested and interesting people will all shape your story. Your desire to share it with others starts as a wish and eventually becomes a main purpose and passion. Your story is special, and someone is waiting to read it and to recognize the lion in you.

Suggestions for Writing Your Book

- **Pick a theme that excites you and can benefit your readers.** Tell your story (autobiographical) or someone else's (biographical). Give important information on how things happened or how they should happen. Share your expertise on how to do something.

- **Create an outline.** Write up a table of contents to guide you. Then break up each chapter into a few sections. Think of your book in terms of its beginning, middle, and end.

- **Get a certain mind-set, method, and motivation.** Raymond Aaron, a *New York Times* best-selling author, said it's possible to write a book with ten chapters in ten weeks and have it published in ten weeks. That's a shortcut to writing a book. This work of fifteen chapters took three years to write, yet 10-10-10 got me started and kept me going.

- **Start small.** Writing three hundred words per day is plenty. Or you can record your thoughts and notes for later transcription and editing.

- **Set a time to work on your book every day.** If you want to take a day or two off per week, schedule that as time off.

- **Choose a set-aside place to write.** This needs to be different from where you do other activities. The idea is to make this a special space so that when you enter it, you're ready to work on your project.

- **Give yourself weekly deadlines.** Choose a word count, percentage of progress—whatever. Just have something to aim for and someone who will hold you accountable.

- **Get early feedback.** Nothing stings worse than writing a book and then having to rewrite it because you didn't let anyone look at it. Have a few trusted advisers help you discern what's worth writing. This helped me to refine my approach, content, and perspective

- **Ship.** No matter what, finish the book, and send it to a publisher or self-publish it. Do whatever you need to do to get it in front of people. Don't just put it in your drawer.
- **Embrace setbacks.** Know that writing a book is hard, and you will mess up. Be okay with it. Give yourself grace. That's what will sustain you, not your standards of perfection.
- **Write another.** So put your work out there, make mistakes, and try again. That's the only way you get good: through practice.

CHAPTER 2

Practice Partnership

Lions live in groups known as prides, which are composed of up to three males and about a dozen females and lion cubs, if the pride has any. A pride's females are generally responsible for hunting so that the pride can eat, and they do so by working together. The male lion's job is to defend the pride's turf. Lions survive in the jungle, where conflict and competition frequently occur. They hunt for food, protect themselves, and lead with authority. Lions teach us the values of partnership and courage.

> *Your First Partnership Begins*
>
> Share one of your earliest experiences of learning to cooperate and work with a family member, friend, or stranger.

My parents, Kaleva and Ines, were great partners who met each other in a memorable way. It was harvest season in the Amasa–Crystal Falls area, and farmers were helping each other to gather grain and other good things. My dad and a group of guys were going with a threshing machine to various farms to help the local folks harvest their oats and barley. Separating the kernels from the chaff resulted in bags of grain that could be stored in grain bins to feed livestock.

One day Kaleva—or Kully, as he was known—went to the Elona Maki farm in a location called Rock Cut. Midway between Amasa and Crystal Falls, this hamlet had a grocery store, elementary school, and home sites around nearby Swan Lake. During a hot workday of considerable dust and sweat, the workmen stopped for a break. The Maki sisters brought food and beverage for them, and Kully and Ines met.

Kully was a good student of life, a creative thinker, and a hard worker, though he never finished high school. Ines was a bright student in school and excelled in math and other subjects. She was enthusiastic and had a good sense of humor. Kully and his brothers and sisters agreed that he could inherit the family farm if he and Ines continued working the Puotinen family farm and provided in-home care for their pioneer parents. Their other sons and daughters moved on to pursue other professions, places, and partners in Lower Michigan, Oregon, Illinois, and Florida. They sometimes returned to the farm, generally in the summertime, to visit their parents, and to attend family reunions.

After my parents were married, they began their life together on the Puotinen family farm. It was a daily challenge to take care of aging parents, cows, and farm chores, as well as their newborn son; I was born in 1941. In a family with such Finnish male names as Elias, Kaleva, Emil, Heino, Eino, Toivo, and Onni, my parents decided to give me the name of Arthur Edwin. They wanted to affirm my identity as a citizen of the United States and help me achieve the opportunities this country afforded me.

Throughout my boyhood years, my parents worked the farm, and I helped. We milked twelve cows by hand twice a day as a threesome. Polka music from the barn radio helped the time pass and the milk flow. In the springtime, Dad and I hauled manure onto the fields and planted potatoes and grain. In the summer, we baled the hay and brought it to the barn, and did other chores. Clay loam soil in the mining district was less fertile and the growing season was shorter than in other states. Picking rocks to get to the potatoes was a lesson in life. We grew a vegetable garden too. Its produce was eaten, stored, canned, and shared with family and friends.

My dad decided to go into partnership with four other farmers to purchase a combine harvester for processing grain in the fields. With this shared asset, they worked together for the common good by harvesting grain, cutting costs, and sharing in the profits. Immigrant Finnish families believed in the cooperative movement, which brought its members into common enterprise, regardless of their political and ideological preferences. The five combine owners were members of different churches and were Democrats and Republicans—and there was one Socialist too.

My parents owned shares in the local consumer cooperative store. Families purchased food and household goods there and took turns manning the store, guided by a full-time manager. The symbol of this combine as a cooperative approach to economic and community life shaped my values and strategies for leadership.

Farm life was a good life though economically challenging. Several cousins from Lower Michigan came in the summer to have fun and help with haying. My parents were advisers to a local 4-H club, organized a softball team of boys and girls, and were youth advisers in our local church. Kully and Ines were friends and mentors to youths and adults alike.

Life was changing too. In earlier decades, when my grandparents were active and their children were growing, the local economy included numerous thriving small farms, productive iron-mining operations, active logging operations, and flourishing families. By the 1950s, some local mines were closing, and those residents with small farms faced a less promising future. My dad was not too active in politics, but he decided one day to write a letter to US representative Gerald Ford of Michigan (later President Ford) to seek help for small farmers. But my mom and dad had to discontinue their farming operation for financial reasons.

Leaders adapt and try new ventures. Ines encouraged everyone she met with her optimism and good spirit. She essentially told Kully to unleash the lion within him, and Kully decided to run for public office as the Crystal Falls township clerk. His marketing approach was to give neighbors his calling card—and some apples and garden vegetables too. He was elected and eventually served for twenty-seven years before retiring at the age of seventy-two. His job included sending out water bills and collecting payments, attending township board meetings, making decisions on property issues, and other administrative matters.

Ines was the unpaid assistant township clerk and helped in many other ways. She was a cook at the Fortune Lake Lutheran Bible Camp in the summers and had a part-time bookkeeping position in Crystal Falls. For many years, she led the Lutheran Church Women's Group at church as its president, the Church Youth Group as its adviser, and the local 4-H club as its director. Her three sisters and their families lived within several miles of each other. The Maki family sisters cared for their families, worked hard, helped one another, and enjoyed life. Ines died at sixty-nine, and my daughter Sara and husband, Scott, have memorialized her life through the Puotinen Family video (see www.room34.com) and Ines's diary.[5]

Ever seeking to make improvements in the community, Kully led efforts to bring township waterlines to homes in place of individual wells. He promoted getting the water supply to a sawmill operation in an outlying area near Amasa. And he traveled to Lansing, Michigan, to present township grant requests for special projects. His passion and persistence provides a landmark example of how to influence decision makers.

Kully unleashed the lion that lived in people as they hoped for better times. Highway 141 extends between the towns of Amasa and Crystal Falls and beyond. The original road wound its way through farming properties, around woods and rock cuts, through Memory Lane trees dedicated to armed service volunteers, and around Dead Man's Curve—a site of several fatal car accidents. Potholes, spring breakup residue, and other inconveniences made for periodic jolts when driving and riding on the road. When I think of my years of riding the school bus to and fro on that twelve-mile stretch, the bumps stand out. Local residents frequently expressed a desire for a new highway, seemingly to no avail.

A breakthrough occurred when a local leader suggested that a delegation of Michigan legislators be invited to visit Crystal Falls and Amasa for a fact-finding opportunity. The five-person team drove more than five hundred miles from the state capitol of Lansing, which included a trip over the Mackinaw Bridge that linked the Upper and Lower Peninsulas of Michigan. The distinguished delegation arrived in time for a special luncheon at the public school in Crystal Falls. They were treated to a hearty meat-pie dish known as a pasty. Cornish miners had brought this food tradition to Michigan, and Finns and other immigrant groups adopted it for their lunch pails when working in the mines or woods, when hunting deer or other game, or whenever.

The creation of a pasty begins with a pie-size crust. You cover half with seasoned potatoes, meat, and other vegetables. You fold over the other half and seal it. The wraparound crust creates a half-moon that is baked and then served piping hot or placed in a lunch pail.

The delegation from Lansing enjoyed the fare in the school dining room and the pie and ice cream that followed. Afterward they took a bumpy school bus ride for the trip back and forth from Crystal Falls to Amasa, experiencing the need for a new road at the gut level. The legislators went back to Lansing and paved the way for new appropriations. Within eighteen months, the new highway was laid, paved, and paid for.

Kully had sparked the team effort to get the new road through Crystal Falls Township. He had hatched the idea to bring the politicians to the people and had worked with others to make the visit happen. When the dedication of the new road took place, others cut the ribbon while he watched with satisfaction on the sidelines.

My grandfather taught me that creativity, persistence, and decisive action are essential to success. Getting the job done is the goal; accolades are secondary. Leadership is a process in which good people working together can make good things happen. My parents' life and legacy in their church and community reflected a vision that involved work and led to victory.

You Learn from Your Parents or Mentors

Take a moment to remember and note how your parents or mentors taught you one or more practices of being a good leader or partner.

Partnership in a family circle is important. Going to school and participating in activities offers many other opportunities to experience cooperation, teamwork, and pride. Lion cubs belong to a pride, or extended family, of adult lions and cubs where social interaction is essential to individual growth and survival. Being an only child presents both limitations and opportunities in growth and development. My aunts, uncles, and cousins helped me learn to interact, cooperate, and care for others. Friends in the community, in the church, and at the local school were important for me too.

Growing up, I didn't want to be lonely or left alone as an only child. Belonging to a team was a breakthrough for me in relation to my social interaction, physical and mental fitness, and leadership skills. My cousins and neighborhood friends liked to play recreational barnyard basketball, softball, and other games when we were not at school or engaged in farm work and other chores.

High school sport teams especially helped me. My class at Crystal Falls High School had only sixty-plus students, so both newcomers and regulars could participate on a team. In my senior year, I was five nine and weighed 165 pounds. My position on the football team offense was center, and Tom Addison, the doctor's son, was the quarterback. Given the times and the size of the team, players often went both ways, so my position on defense was left linebacker. A new coach came to the school in my sophomore year, and he turned the football program around. Dick Mettlach taught us football fundamentals as well as play and defensive strategies that succeeded. Above all, he believed in teamwork, in never giving up, and in good sportsmanship.

Coaches and football teams are measured by results. The Crystal Falls Trojans went undefeated in my junior and senior years in Class D football. Some of my friends made All Upper Peninsula classification. I was honorable mention and a cocaptain of our team. Dick Mettlach coached for several decades and took teams to the Class D finals year after year, earning the title of state champ or runner-up. Being part of his team meant the discipline of daily practice, the prodding of perceptive coaching, and the *wow* of winning.

Playing high school basketball was a mixed blessing for. Several football players were also on the basketball team, and my jump shot beyond the arc was acceptable enough for me to start as a point guard in my junior year. However, in midseason, my right ankle was sprained, my self-confidence waned, and the coach placed me in the second string. This setback prodded me to focus on long-term priorities, such as my studies and my plans to study for a career in ministry.

In my first year of college, I experienced a new type of coach: Professor Arthur Hill, director of the Suomi College Choir. He blended talented voices with newcomers to the choir into an ensemble of forty voices that toured regionally and on the East Coast. He took an alumni choir to Finland three years later—my first overseas travel experience. It was exciting and educational. My initial choir experience as a first tenor brought me new joy, as did the soprano soloist, Sandra Tamminen, my first love. In our sophomore year, she turned her attention to another Suomi student. Thereafter, my leadership responsibilities as student body president and my studies required my talents and emphasis.

After my transfer as a junior student to Augustana College in Illinois, Dr. Henry Veld, director of the college's choir, became my director and vocal teacher. The discipline of his rehearsals and his persistent pursuit of a perfect sound from blended voices made him an exemplar of achieving joy and beauty in music. He would remark that he had heard the perfect sound one time, during four measures of a concert he had conducted in rural Illinois. High standards of performance and a legato singing style were his forte.

You Join with Teammates

Share here one or more important values you gained from teamwork and partnership in school and college.

22

Your on-the-job training, experiential education, and other opportunities for leadership development help you attain your vision and goals. For me, valuable team-building experiences took place in Hickory, North Carolina. The president of Lenoir-Rhyne College, Dr. Albert Anderson, hired me in 1978 as his academic vice president. He was a Harvard-trained scholar in philosophy who loved nature and the North woods in Minnesota.

Anderson obtained a grant so that the administrative team and selected staff and faculty could participate in a nine-day Outward Bound program in North Carolina. When the first team returned, he and several colleagues told the campus community about their adventures. He told us how people from various regions in the United States came together to experience various so-called initiatives that tested personal strengths, group interaction, spirituality, and persistence. Lenoir-Rhyne representatives were separated and placed in different teams that consisted of ten participants led by two instructors.

They each detailed a particularly challenging activity, known as a "crux" moment. Anderson's crux moment occurred when his team took turns navigating a ropes course between trees in the forest. One by one, team members walked across a single log suspended in the air. A young woman walked surely and confidently across the log. A college football player was unable to take even the first step. Anderson said he made it part of the way—and then this existentialist philosopher had a decision to make. He could not freeze in his tracks forever. He did not want to turn back and fail the test. Nor did he want to fall from the log. Instead he slowly forged ahead with faith. This type of crux experience for leaders occurs in all kinds of settings and situations. Experiences like those on Outward Bound prepare you for later challenges that test your physical, emotional, and spiritual limits.

My turn came several weeks later at an Outward Bound Base Camp just south of Ashville, North Carolina. My team of ten members was mainly young male and female professionals from various states and a graduate student from Poland, preparing to be a medical doctor. We were an attorney, a marketing executive from Wall Street, and students. Our lean and fit male and female instructors guided us. Bonded initially by their command, we chose to adapt, achieve, and work together as a team.

The Outward Bound program tests and extends physical, mental, and social limits. Instructors direct group initiatives and activities, such as rock climbing and rappelling, going through a suspended ropes course, whitewater rafting, and runs, solitary overnight stays in the woods, a several-day backpacking expedition, and other adventures. In the process, you learn the strengths and limitations of each member and help one another.

Our expedition hiked to the top of Rabun Bald, the highest peak in Georgia. Team members took turns in leading the orienteering, the walk, and the preparations. The best backpacker and walk guide was a cocktail waitress and backhoe operator from Boise, Idaho. She was unable to complete the ropes course, but she led our group in the final hours to the top of Rabun Bald as we bushwhacked our way through thick rhododendron and underbrush.

It was early morning of the third day when we reached the observation platform on Rabun Bald. The sun was shining and the wind gently blowing. We saw four different states on the horizon. This aha experience was monumental. Two thoughts came to mind: I could not do this trek alone, and together as a team we struggled and succeeded. (See www.outwardbound.org for additional information on this leadership training experience in several locations in the United States and elsewhere.)[6]

> *You Reach the Top Together*
>
> Share a time when you and your team worked together to reach a new level of achievement.

Life and work experiences are building blocks for advancement in your career. Add one more block: continuing education. After several years at Lenoir-Rhyne College, my career assessment led me to studies in leadership and skill building as a pathway to a college presidency. I was primarily educated in the humanities and had done no coursework in business, accounting, and economics, so it was important for me to gain new strengths and skills in these areas.

After completing several prerequisite undergraduate courses in those fields in the Lenoir-Rhyne College summer school program, I applied to enroll in the executive MBA program at Wake Forest University in Winston-Salem, North Carolina. Upon my acceptance in 1982, Wake Forest University business professors taught my class of forty-five students in a two-year degree program that featured four courses per semester. Classes alternated weekly between Fridays and Saturdays. Lenoir-Rhyne allowed me to do this study while maintaining my regular duties as academic dean.

Once a week, three fellow students from Hickory, North Carolina, and I traveled to Winston-Salem for our class sessions. The MBA program organized students into teams of four to six participants. My team partners were younger professionals in their thirties from different career fields, and my commuting partners were among them. Our study team met together one midweek night, collaborating in our studies and preparing group presentations for the entire class. We learned from each other and from professors with significant educational, career, and business experience in various fields.

During the first year of my MBA studies, Anderson left his post to accept a strategic planning and development vice presidential position at Luther College in Iowa. Thereafter the acting president began his tenure at a dollar-a-year salary. This local business leader and member of the Lenoir-Rhyne board of trustees gifted the college with business acumen and decisive decision making. He fired the football coach during midseason, released a long-time member of the library staff, and made other personnel decisions.

One day he informed me that my position was not renewed for the following fall semester in order to allow the new president to bring in his own academic dean. The presidential selection process had bypassed my application and that of another talented Lenoir-Rhyne administrator to go outside the campus community for a new president.

You Lose Your Position

Remember a time when you were denied a promotion or let go and what you did after receiving the news.

My family was forced to plan a relocation move during my search for a new position in the remaining four months of my contract. It was my first experience of that kind of rejection. After considering my several options with my wife and daughters, I declined the offers of two vice presidential opportunities at a college in Buffalo, New York, and a college in Chicago for two main reasons: I wanted to remain in Lutheran higher education and to complete my MBA program at Wake Forest University.

Fortunately President Norm Fintel of Roanoke College in Salem, Virginia, invited me to be his associate dean of academic affairs and to continue my MBA studies. My travel on alternating Fridays and

Saturdays was a solo adventure, going over the Blue Ridge Parkway in the Smoky Mountains to and from Winston-Salem, driving my yellow 1971 Karman Ghia and listening to music tapes.

The two-year program was worth it. My new knowledge and skills in such fields as macroeconomics, advanced accounting, strategic planning, negotiation, marketing, entrepreneurship, and human resource management added expertise. My professors were excellent mentors and teachers, and my MBA team members gave me encouragement and information to move ahead. Earning the MBA degree in 1984 enabled me to progress in my academic career and to use my knowledge and skills in team building in local, regional, and national situations.

The one-year experience in Salem benefited our family of five. Judy obtained a special-education teaching position, and our three young daughters progressed in their studies, with Anne receiving several academic awards in her junior year in high school. My major contribution to Roanoke College for that year was to lead a task force on student retention that developed new strategies for teaching and supporting both underachieving and gifted students.

Your experiences with teams are essential to developing strong leadership, so we conclude this chapter with some ways to work effectively with a team.

Suggestions for Building a Strong Team

- **Share a common vision.** The team leader and all team members play a role in identifying a common vision that unifies the team.
- **Bring out the best** in the variety of skills and personalities among the team. Good teamwork occurs when all team

27

members maximize their strengths, help other team members, and overcome challenges together.

- **Build trust between team members.** Trust comes through knowing each other and having positive experiences together. New teams benefit from team-building activities that focus on building trust.
- **Involve the team in decision making.** Robust dialogue among team members about ideas, action options, and desired outcomes fosters ownership in making decisions and follow-through efforts.
- **Be open with information sharing** among team members on possibilities, projects, and problems. Creativity, collaboration, and cooperation lead to success.
- **Provide recognition and rewards for team members.** Value everyone's contributions, and distribute resources to members fairly. Explore personal and group incentives for performance.
- **Go out as a team** so you get to know each other outside the workplace, such as at a sporting event or lunch in a local park or restaurant. Or participate as a team in a corporate challenge or team charity event. Or have an Outward Bound experience.

CHAPTER 3

Speak Up

A distinctive feature of a lion is its voice. The male lion roars with authority and power to mark his territory. His voice can carry up to five miles in flat terrain. Roars last between thirty to forty seconds. Females also roar, and their roars are generally much softer and higher in pitch. Pride members recognize each other's roars. So a lion learns how to use its voice in various circumstances for effect, such as to call a pride member, warn a predator, or roar before a fight.

Humans have a voice for communication. You talk every day with people in a variety of situations, and you connect by varying your voice. Your compassionate voice expresses care for another person. Your enthusiastic voice conveys energy and enthusiasm. Your courageous voice conveys resolve and strength. Situational analysis and personal feelings guide which voice you choose. Leaders speak up at the right time with the right words.

President John F. Kennedy wrote a book entitled *Profiles in Courage* that tells of the courageous voices and actions of notable American leaders. A profile in courage himself, Kennedy elevated the hopes and aspirations of many Americans with his stirring speeches. With conviction and resolve he proclaimed, "Ask not what your country can do for you; rather ask what you can do for your country."

Martin Luther King gave his "I Have a Dream" speech in Washington at a key point in the civil rights struggle, and it is remembered today for its lasting vision and because of his courage in the face of imminent danger.

Alfredo Alvarez, a civil rights attorney in Des Moines, Iowa, spoke to a group of honor students. In his youth, he had a stuttering problem, and he wanted to speak with clarity and persuasiveness. His speech teacher encouraged him to practice speaking by reciting the speeches of famous people. He borrowed a library book with such speeches, walked into an Iowa cornfield, and spoke them again and again. Alfredo discovered his courageous voice. His oral presentation of his work to help Latino Americans in legal matters was effective and memorable for those who heard it.

Leaders practice speaking, choose the right words, and reach out to others with purpose and persuasiveness. Your communication occurs in a family circle, a group gathering, and before an audience.

You Learn to Roar

Share how you felt when you spoke before a group to present an important message.

Being hesitant, indecisive, or inconclusive makes your presentation less effective. Each person needs to discover and develop his or her voice, and here's my journey to speak persuasively:

My public-speaking experiences extend over forty years. They include speaking in such settings as local churches, classrooms, fundraising appeals, government groups, international settings, and both small groups and hundreds of listeners. My purpose is to inform and inspire listeners and to enjoy hearing and learning from other speakers.

Living in a rural area of Upper Michigan, my family valued our heritage of faith, work, and resourcefulness. My church and public school opened windows to a larger world and doorways to growth in knowledge and service. In my junior year in Crystal Falls High School, I felt the call to study for the ministry, and my pastor, Wilbert "Sully" Ruohomaki, encouraged me to preach a sermon one Sunday during his summer vacation. It was based on the story Jesus told about the rich man and Lazarus (Luke 16:19–31). My message was entitled "From Rags and Riches to Righteousness."

In my high school, as class valedictorian and student body president I gave a short speech during the commencement exercises. I had rewritten it several times and practiced it in the field while tending to our farm animals. It was far less memorable than the speech given by Dr. Harold Sponberg, president of Eastern Michigan University. His talk contained one compelling sentence that he illustrated with persuasive examples and a unifying challenge: "You can be a builder."

After two years at Suomi College in Hancock, my undergraduate studies continued at Augustana College in Rock Island, Illinois. It was my first time far away from home. I boarded the train in Amasa with two suitcases. One contained my clothing; the other carried my Bible, my notebook with goals for my college experience, and other essentials. It was my "suitcase of dreams."

The transfer in Chicago to the Rock Island train brought me to Augustana College, where the experiences exceeded my expectations. My professors—Louis Almen, George Arbaugh, Peter Beckman, Ross Paulson, and others—opened new vistas of knowledge in history, philosophy, and religion for me.

After my college graduation, other learned lions beckoned. Dean Ted Conrad of the Lutheran School of Theology at the Chicago–Rock Island Campus welcomed me to seminary studies by saying, "You have come here with many talents, and we will help you sharpen your skills." The school was nicknamed "The School of the Prophets" and emphasized developing skills for proclamation, pastoral care, and mission in the world. Many memorable mentors guided me, including Arthur Arnold in preaching, G. Everett Arden in church history, Arnold Carlson in theology, Paul Swanson in pastoral care, and Robert Benne in ethics. They provided a breadth and depth of knowledge shared in a variety of settings. The interaction among students also enriched my growth and development.

Dr. Arnold commented in a preaching class one day, "Remember, it's not what you say but what the people hear that is most important." Each sermon, with its theme, illustrations, and call to action, seeks to connect with the spiritual needs and expectations of listeners. The love of God for every person is the foundation for building strong relationships with other people. Awareness of and belief in divine and human love creates the vision and energy for good people to work together to make good things happen.

In college years, the blessing of finding a mate gives new meaning to partnership, pride, and passion. Judy Cathleen Kapoun and I began dating after a college and community choir rehearsal of Handel's *Messiah* at Augustana College. She was from West Saint Paul, Minnesota. As young couples do, we dreamed and talked about our future. A year later, on February 29, 1964, I made a leap-year move. On a hill overlooking the bell tower that evening, I gave my marriage proposal to Judy in English, Finnish, and German. She agreed, and I made three promises. "If we work together and help each other, we can be a college presidential family someday. I promise to take you to Europe, and there you can purchase china and tableware, as you will host many people in our home."

32

We were married that August. And the three promises were fulfilled, although delayed until twenty-four years later. A dream deferred is not a dream denied. I refer to that presidential dream in a later chapter.

You Declare Your Love

Share a time when you spoke memorable words of love to your partner, family member or dear friend.

During my second year at Rock Island, Judy began her teaching career in Davenport, Iowa. As a newly married couple, we enjoyed getting to know and value the other married couples and students at the seminary. Building friendships and our marriage partnership gave added meaning and excitement to our life.

As an important step in becoming an ordained pastor, the third internship year of seminary study involved placement in a Lutheran congregation with supervision by the local pastor in guided learning experiences in most phases of parish ministry. Administration, faculty, and pastors of local congregations collaborated in the selection process, and we classmates expectantly waited for our assignments. My internship in Omaha, Nebraska, was particularly challenging.

In August of 1965, Judy and I moved to Omaha for my internship year at Augustana Lutheran Church, near Creighton University, and for her new teaching position at Minne Lusa Elementary School. The parish pastor, L. William Youngdahl, was the son of former Minnesota governor Luther Youngdahl and shared his father's passion for social justice. In 1963 Youngdahl had come to Omaha from New York after experiences in social ministry at the national level of the Lutheran Church in America. His Swedish American heritage and talents endeared him to the largely Swedish American congregation.

After building relationships and caring for congregational members, Youngdahl envisioned developing communications between the Augustana church and another local Lutheran congregation comprised of many African Americans. Lutheran Film Associates of New York learned of his outreach to the community and contacted him about filming a documentary of the new project. It would be an unscripted film using *cinema verite* (true to life) methodology to depict conversations, emotions, and actions as they unfolded.

"Burn, baby, burn" was a catchphrase at the time in certain sections of cities such as Detroit and Chicago. However, the framers of this film sought a Middle American, Midwestern city and a traditional Lutheran congregation facing the challenge of improving race relations among community residents. My internship began several weeks before the film crew, led by Bill Jersey, arrived in early October to begin the filming process.[7]

Jersey focused on three primary stories. He wanted some scenes of Youngdahl meeting with Ernie Chambers in his barbershop. The encounter involved the pastor primarily listening to this articulate African American leader holding forth while cutting a client's hair. He persuasively made the case for social justice for African Americans. He also pointed out the reality of racism in the attitudes and actions of white Omaha residents and their organizations, including the church. Chambers later ran for office in the Nebraska legislature and served there for many years.

A second story line followed the efforts of Youngdahl in meetings with the Augustana church council and selected committees to lay the groundwork for his proposal. Youngdahl and the pastor of the African American congregation agreed to initiate several interracial visits among the members. They envisioned small-group exchange visits at Sunday morning worship, Sunday school sessions for high school youth, home visits, and other initiatives. Some Augustana church leaders were initially reticent to launch the program, but the high school study group exchange began while Jersey filmed the action.

On Reformation Sunday in late October, it was my turn to be the preacher at Augustana Lutheran Church. The high school representatives from both congregations were in attendance, and my message proclaimed that freedom in Christ meant that Christians should be open to new ways of ministry, including shared efforts by both congregations to strengthen community service. This section of my part in the film ended up on the cutting-room floor. The Monday after the service featured a film clip of Youngdahl and me discussing the current situation in the congregation. He posed the question "Do you believe we should go ahead with the study group initiatives involving both congregations?" My reply was to wait and work for a consensus among the congregational members before proceeding. Did this lion lack courage? Or was he being strategic?

Resistance among some Augusta Lutheran members grew in opposition to Youngdahl's efforts. However, a filmmaker and member in the congregation, Ray Christensen, led a support group for Youngdahl and spoke many memorable lines in the film. Whereas burning of buildings or other urban riot scenes occurred elsewhere, the issues of conscience and conflict engulfed the congregation. As the weeks wore on, Youngdahl lost the support of Bishop Reuben Swanson. At the annual meeting of the congregation in January, Youngdahl resigned his pastorate. He subsequently moved on to other Lutheran positions at Augsburg College in Minneapolis and a pastorate in the Berkeley, California, area before joining the United Church of Christ denomination.

Marshall Foch said that the most powerful force is a soul on fire, and my internship experience lit a spark. Dealing with conflicts henceforth became a priority in my research and writing and in my administrative and pastoral positions.

You Take a Stand

Share a time when you spoke up in a group setting about your views on a controversial issue.

When I returned to Rock Island, Illinois, in 1966 for my senior year in seminary, other tests of leadership awaited me, for the student body had elected me as its president. Classroom and informal discussions often dealt with the role of clergy in the civil rights movement and the Vietnam conflict. A national movement known as Clergy and Laity Concerned about Vietnam gained momentum in 1966–67, and it issued an appeal for conscientious people to rally in Washington, DC, and to give public expression to their views.[8] Interest grew among our seminary students to send a delegation to Washington and to use student organization funds to assist with the team's travel expenses.

The matter came to a vote at a student-body meeting in the seminary cafeteria. Voices were heard for and against the "send the LSTC delegation to DC" proposal. When the votes were counted, they were split fifty/fifty, and the president needed to cast the deciding vote. I voted to send our seminary delegation to Washington. Judy had given birth to our firstborn daughter, Anne Marie, a few weeks before, so I opted not to be part of the delegation. Those classmates that did go returned with a resolve to continue seeking ways to resolve the Vietnam conflict.

The war in Vietnam had an impact on our family. After my graduation from LSTC in Rock Island in May of 1967, our emerging family of three moved to Chicago for my first year of master's and doctoral studies at the University of Chicago Divinity School.

Judy's brother Timothy was drafted into the army during his fall semester break at the University of Minnesota. After basic training, he was sent to the battlefields of the Mekong Delta. His first letters graphically described the daily dangers he faced as a radio operator in his platoon. Within a few weeks, he was declared missing in action, which of course was a major blow to his parents, John and Orliss, and his siblings, Judy, Patricia, and James. Other family members and friends felt the stress of this situation, which extended for many months.

On March 31, 1968, my ordination into the Lutheran ministry took place in my home church in Amasa. This small country church felt the impact of larger world news; it was the same day President Lyndon Johnson announced that he would not seek reelection. My pastorate at Trinity Lutheran Church on Wilson Avenue in Chicago began in the summer of 1968 during the tumultuous Democratic Party Convention. At the Lutheran Church in America Illinois Synod Assembly meeting that year, its delegates were divided on the resolution of support or nonsupport of United States involvement in the Vietnam conflict.

On national TV, Walter Cronkite gave the daily headcount of the US service personnel who died in the war, and each statistic was a story of its own. One fateful day, US Army personnel came to the Kapoun family home in West Saint Paul to inform them that Tim's body was being sent home for burial after being missing in action for more than a year. Soon after, our family gathered for his memorial services in his home church to celebrate Tim's courageous life. His body was interred at Fort Snelling in Saint Paul. Years later his father, a World War II veteran, requested that his own ashes be placed at the gravesite of his son and that the family gather there to honor his wishes.

Like many other soldiers, Tim unleashed his courage to go into battle, and his death made an impression on us. Judy was an experienced elementary education teacher and later specialized in special education and learning disabilities. Tim had learning disabilities, and Judy dedicated herself to working with this special group of students because she saw Tim in so many of them. My doctoral thesis was dedicated in his honor.

You Mourn Their Passing

Share a time when you expressed words of comfort to a family that lost a loved one.

Memorable speeches are needed during times of death and grief. There are many other occasions when good words aptly spoken can be joyful and celebratory, such as graduations, weddings, and awards banquets. On the other hand, one-on-one sales presentations need to be persuasive and beneficial to all concerned.

Preparing a speech or other communication begins with identifying its purpose. Do you intend to entertain, to inform, or to call for some type of action? Will a theme or story be developed in the message? What is the structure and content of the message, such as one compelling thought or three main points? Will you use notes or PowerPoint or a dramatic presentation in your message? Will you speak without notes, which is an act of courage? Will you stand up unprepared and just speak what comes to mind? A preacher at a Prayer Breakfast in Washington sermonized by saying, "I just stand in the pulpit and wait for the Holy Spirit to send me the message, and I grab the thunderbolts as they come whistling by." Discovering your own style that communicates well is important. A message involving both your intellect and your emotions is more apt to reach and touch your audience.

My own speaking style has evolved. As a college professor, my teaching moved from the lecture method to interactive communication and problem solving with students. Coaches and mentors use this style in workshops related to business and self-development. As a college dean and president, I offered important information regarding educational practices in our learning community, and many of my presentations were intended to build relationships with donors, volunteers, and others. In various educational and church settings, my messages became shorter—twelve to fifteen minutes. It generally included a biblical story, historical and contemporary illustrations, and references to events and people from the congregation, personal examples, and a persuasive call to a focused action. Oral practice sessions generally preceded my presentations.

More recently a "sunshine report" or brief humorous story has become part of my opening announcements or my sermon. People come to a worship service with varying levels of interest and expectation as well as the burden of cares, worries, and fears. The lighter touch helps set people at ease for the message that follows. I first used this approach at First Lutheran Church in Iron River, Michigan, in 2002. Our worship service was a live radio broadcast transmitted over a forty-mile radius to a fairly remote area. A homebound parishioner encouraged me to start the "sunshine report," and it was received well, both in Michigan and in my parish in Elgin, Illinois. Here was my first sunshine report, a well-traveled story:

> A burglar broke into a house one night. He shone his flashlight around, looking for valuables. When he picked up a CD player to place in his sack, a strange, disembodied

voice echoed from the dark, saying, "Jesus is watching you." He nearly jumped out of his skin, clicked his flashlight out, and froze.

When he heard nothing more after a bit, he shook his head, clicked the light back on, and began searching for more valuables. Just as he pulled the stereo out so he could disconnect the wires, he heard, clear as a bell, "Jesus is watching you." Freaked out, he shone his light around frantically, looking for the source of the voice. Finally, in the corner of the room, his flashlight beam came to rest on a parrot.

"Did you say that?" he hissed at the parrot.

"Yep," the parrot confessed. "I'm just trying to warn you."

The burglar relaxed. "Warn me, huh? Who the hell are you?"

"Moses," replied the bird.

"Moses!" The burglar laughed. "What kind of stupid people would name a parrot Moses?"

"Probably the same kind of people that would name a Rottweiler Jesus," the bird answered.

Members began e-mailing me or telling me of sunshine reports, so it became a participatory event for pastor and members alike. My brand emerged of being a good-humored person that liked to bring hope and good cheer to others along with serious, deeper elements of spirituality.

You Make a Lasting Impression

Remember a time when your presentation to a group was perceived to be informative, entertaining, and/or helpful.

Every speaker develops a personal style, and here are some suggestions to consider in preparing and giving your next memorable speech. You have the power of mind, heart, and spirit to do so.

Suggestions for Speaking to Groups

- **Believe that you have a story to tell,** a message to be heard, and a cause to champion. People need to benefit from your knowledge and wisdom, your courage and compassion.
- **Seek opportunities to give your message** in your workplace or school, in local community organizations, on multimedia, and in other settings.
- **Prepare it rather than wing it**. Read or listen to others speakers on your subject. Develop one or more creative ways to present your material. Write out notes or a manuscript; go over it orally several times. Make changes as needed.
- **Be ready to step forward with courage when your time comes.** Rev up your readiness and breathe deeply—it's show time. For sermons, I pray for the power of the Holy Spirit to work through me to bring God's message. You may notice when attending seminars or other events that many speakers walk forward quickly to the podium. Enthusiasm, excitement, and energy are essential to making a good impression and to developing the flow of your message.
- **Start with a bang.** The first thirty seconds have the most impact. Don't waste these precious seconds with "Ladies and

Gentlemen" or a weather report. Come out punching with a startling statement, quote, or story.

- **Observe the facial expressions and body language of your audience** during your speech, and make adaptations as needed. What do you do when a baby starts to cry, a cell phone goes off, or a listener asks one question after another?
- **Structure your information.** You and your audience will remember your points better if you have a clear outline. For example, start by saying, "Here are the five questions I'm asked most."
- **Use handouts or overheads.** If your presentation involves statistics and analytical data, put them in a handout or an overhead that the audience can refer to. Don't bore your listeners by reciting a plethora of numbers. Stories are what make a talk memorable and lively.
- **Remember to roar with enthusiasm.** Speak clearly so you can be heard. And enjoy your moment in the sun or spotlight.
- **Humor helps.** Real-life humorous incidents, stories, or jokes can be adapted into your own style. Some speakers start with the sunshine; others shine later in their message.

CHAPTER 4

Roam Your Territory

Mountain lions establish territories, which they mark and guard. Males establish larger territories than females, and a male's territory may overlap that of several females. Territories range from forty to eighty square miles for males and twenty to thirty square miles for females. When a mountain lion establishes a territory, he or she is referred to as the "resident."

Humans establish their personal territories too, such as the neighborhoods where they live, the communities where they work, and the networks where they connect with family, friends, clients, and others. Technology has expanded the types of networks that a person can explore and become a "resident" of.

You Expand Your Network

Note the different ways you keep in contact with family, friends, mentors, colleagues, clients, and associates.

Have you wanted to explore and establish a new territory that can change your life? Have you ever wanted to host your own radio show, for example? It can happen for you as it did for me. One way to explore new territory is to have a good partner to work with, someone who knows what to do. WMPL radio station in Hancock had an owner/broadcaster named Bob Olson. He became a marathon runner after losing weight and giving up smoking. He went on to do ultramarathons, running up to fifty miles a day for a week or two at a time. He ran the Boston Marathon several times and then decided with a friend to run halfway around Lake Superior one summer and the other halfway route the next summer. Hence Bob became known as "Super Body" Bob Olson.

In the 1970s in the Copper Country of Upper Michigan, Bob cofounded a local radio station with a signal spanning the range of a mountain lion—forty to eighty square miles. He established this region as his territory by pioneering the "people power" radio concept, which featured live interviews with guests in the station or off-site about a variety of subjects. It became a lively way of connecting people on the air as conversations among many voices covered a variety of concerns.

During the live broadcasts, Bob would phone certain people in outlying areas that reported on community events, used items for sale or trade, and local weather conditions. My cousin Esther Lahti lived in a small locale named Herman and became known as the "weather lady" for she gave regular reports of snow depths and climate changes in one of the coldest spots in the territory.

Bob was an avid sports fan and broadcast live reports on the basketball, ice hockey, and football games of Michigan Technology University and local high schools. One year, the winter snow was a little late in coming for the skiing and snowmobile enthusiasts, so he had a local musician create and record the "Heikki Lunta" song. (That's Finnish for Hank Snow.) Bob began playing it many times a day to awaken Mother Nature to send snow to the area, and sometimes it seemed to help.

Bob's radio station offered many types of programs with a variety of familiar voices. National, regional, and local news reports were daily fare. WMPL covered local events and interviewed people in the news. These and other programs reflected the "people power" brand, which emphasized community pride, resourcefulness, and citizen involvement.

When my academic deanship at Suomi College began in 1974, I sought ways to expand the concept of recording personal and communal heritage, I believed a radio interview program could complement the one-on-one interviews being done for the college's Finnish Folklore and Social Change Oral History Project. Bob and I decided to create a Wednesday-afternoon talk show that would be on air for an hour or more. We called it the "Heritage Line" with community heritage as the focus and line being the radio technology of instant access and open participation by call-in commentators.

Bob and I cohosted the show. We contacted several participants before and during the program, and he managed the program flow with occasional commercials. Each program had a theme with an occasional studio guest and an invitation for listeners to call in. Occasional commercials by area businesses underwrote the program costs of WMPL, and volunteer participation, including my time, made the Heritage Line a low-cost addition to the lineup of radio programs.

Our first broadcast was on Copper Country winters, and folks called in stories about the year that over three hundred inches of snow fell in the area. Other programs dealt with mining and logging, education and sports, folk medicine and family life, and many other topics. Our purpose was to gather information and foster pride in local residents regarding their history and heritage. Bob recorded the Heritage Line program, and I brought the tapes to the Finnish

American Immigrant Archives of Suomi College for use by students, scholars, and other interested people.

In a memorable interview, we phoned Evert Jurmu, a cook in a lumber camp. In getting his story that day, we unleashed a lion in Evert as he exuberantly recalled how some lumberjacks ate as many as five pork chops for breakfast. Another lumberman, Swande Goodell, joined us for a few weeks as a studio guest, helping interview other loggers in the area. As a finale to this series, we organized a luncheon at Suomi College for retired lumbermen, loggers, and others. They enjoyed getting together and celebrating their work in a logging industry that continues today in the region.

The Heritage Line program was a hoot to do. We heard important information, listened to some tall tales, and enjoyed ethnic humor. With forty different nationalities represented over the years in the Copper Country, we featured programs on Cornish humor, Irish humor, Finnish humor, and others. The Heritage Line became a favorite for many people because it built community pride, preserved local history in a folk medium, and featured many local citizens. The program had public-relations value for Suomi College and my own brand as a regional historian with expertise in the Finnish American experience.

You Enjoy Your Media Moment

Share a time that you were on a radio or TV program and what you learned from that event.

The lore of the Lake Superior region had become my personal pool of discovery. My aspirations, values, and talents flourished in my family and work-related relationships. Our youngest daughter, Sara, was born in 1974 and became Judy's daily companion for her physical education workouts at the Paavo Nurmi Physical Education Center. Anne and Marji did well in school and enjoyed their playmates. My parents lived only ninety miles away at the Puotinen family farm, and Judy's parents were only a day's drive away in the Twin Cities.

In 1964, Judy and I still shared a dream with three promises. To position myself to become a future college president, I needed further administrative experience in a four-year college. So I began a selective search for such a position.

When I was called to be the academic vice president of Lenoir-Rhyne College in Hickory, North Carolina, in 1978, we moved to a new region with its own ethnic and educational traditions. Fortunately the Heritage Line continued in good hands with Bob and my colleague at Suomi College, Olaf Rankinen. Fluent in English and Finnish, Olaf served in several leadership positions in the Lutheran church, including a term with the Lutheran Association of Missionary Pilots (LAMP). Olaf was a certified pilot, and in LAMP he regularly flew a one-engine airplane from High Level, Canada, to remote locations to conduct worship and other pastoral services. He once described how he learned to fly in whiteout situations in a snowstorm. Olaf was a model of courageous leadership.

You Start a New Show

You and a friend discuss several topics or formats for a talk show. Which ideas do you wish to develop?

When one chapter in life ends and another begins, an old adage holds true: "We never forget how to ride a bike." Ten years later, in 1988, an opportunity to cohost a new radio program occurred during my term as president of Grand View College in Des Moines. Its newest academic building, the Cowles Communication Center, included a TV studio, radio station, photography lab, classrooms, and faculty offices.

The staff assistant for the faculty and students at the communication center was a friendly and vivacious woman named Diane Schaefer. During our initial campus visit for presidential candidate interviews, she guided Judy and me around the campus on the coldest day of the year. Diane also brought her upbeat, positive spirit to the newly developing Union Park Neighborhood Association around the Grand View campus. We both were among the founding members of this group.

Diane and I developed the Grand View Good Neighbors Show for several reasons. We wanted to promote the East Side community and its citizens. We also wanted to recognize local leaders in various walks of life who were contributing to the common good. We showcased some of our faculty, staff, and administrators as well as students. We also invited studio guests that served in leadership positions on the Grand View College board of trustees and its development board.

The earlier radio show, Heritage Line, had been a weekly with phone conversations and walk-on guests in our studio right on the main street of Hancock. The Grand View Good Neighbors Show was more controlled because of scheduling, a smaller studio, and a lack of phone-call interaction with the listening public. Nonetheless, the program worked well. We identified a community or college interview guest who agreed to join Diane and me in the small studio. A Grand View student served as recording engineer. We prerecorded a half-hour program in the radio station for later broadcast on the next Tuesday evening. Our interview format was basic: Tell us about you. What work do you do? How are you a good neighbor in this community?

Enthusiastic and charming, Diane was the right-brain side of our team; my selection of interviewees and questions posed reflected my left-brain leaning. We created good will for the college by hosting community leaders on the program. We interviewed current and future board members and several people high on our development fund list. We talked to faculty and staff members and coaches. We occasionally included international leaders, such as the interpreter for Mikhail Gorbachev, who assisted in his negotiations with President Ronald Reagan. This interpreter spoke at a local civic club, was interviewed on our Good Neighbors program, and became an overnight guest at my home. Another important guest was Preston Daniels, who led a local community organization, became a city council member, and was later elected as the first African American mayor in Des Moines. He recalled taking summer courses at Grand View and receiving important encouragement and coaching in speaking before he went on to earning his degrees at Drake University.

The Good Neighbor program showcased local leaders. Some guests had experienced radio interviews in other venues, but for many it was a first-time experience. Being valued and recognized is important for people, and Diane had a charming way of making it enjoyable for them. For me, this radio show became a good way to get better acquainted with community leaders, current and future college leaders, and donors. The program conveyed that we cared about the community and its future, and it received a special award from a national organization. Diane and I never attempted to determine the number of weekly listeners we had, yet we could report that some of our guests became trustees, alumni, and development leaders as well as contributors.

In March 1990, American Women in Radio and Television bestowed the Good Neighbor program its honorable mention in the National AWRT Commendation Awards, in recognition of excellence in programming that presents a positive and realistic portrayal of women.

You Interview Major Leaders

Identify three or more leaders in your community that you wish to interview to help you in some way. Contact and interview them.

Today the large variety of media channels and outlets opens more opportunities for both professionals and amateurs to host their own radio shows, TV programs, or telecommunications events. Expanding your personal horizon is now possible because social media extends the reach of your influence, the sound of your voice, and your network of contacts. With an Internet connection, your own website, and media devices, you can reach a greater circle of friends, network of business clientele, and audience of readers, listeners, and collaborators. You can do a twenty- to thirty-minute interview on your own YouTube site. As you progress, you can offer a two- to three-day live, continuing-education event, workshop, or boot camp. Sample topics include leadership training, real-estate investing, writers' workshops, and branding and marketing. In preparation for this book, my online contacts led me to many transformational authors, teleseminars, digital books, and free resources. Many of these examples are readily accessible, inexpensive, and very informative.

Suggestions for Reaching a Greater Audience

- **Get started.** Watch and listen to some successful radio and TV hosts. Observe how they conduct interviews. Visit a radio studio and ask questions about doing interviews. Be interviewed by a radio host. Do some practice interviews with a colleague and friend about a subject or two. Ask basic questions: How did you get started in your life's work? What are you doing now that is exciting and rewarding?

- **Develop a concept for a radio show.** Build on a subject or theme that excites you and energizes interviewees and listeners. Heritage Line and Grand View Good Neighbors exemplify that idea.

- **Work with a partner.** Linking with an experienced interviewer or expert in your concept area is helpful. Bob Olson and Diane Schaefer are good examples, and you can find someone too. With technology advances, you can do your interviews in webinars and tele series, and bring online partners to assist you.

- **Be personable with a real personality.** Seek to bring out the best in your radio guests. Have some flair about you as you ask questions and they offer information. Enjoy them and their perspectives. Share humor and human-interest stories. What is it about them that you enjoy?

- **Know your subject.** Obtain some biographical information about your guests, and make a preliminary contact to determine topics they would like to discuss or you would like to discuss with them. Do additional homework for in-depth interviews. Each Heritage Line show focused on a particular topic. In the Grand View Good Neighbors program, we asked three questions of a single guest, which led to productive half-hour interviews.

- **Listen to learn.** An interview is supposed to be a two-way conversation. You ask a question; you get a response. Some hosts get carried away with talking and allow little time for guests to say what they have to say. Don't talk just to hear yourself talk.

- **Always have a backup plan.** What would you do if a guest canceled the day of your show? Would you cancel your show or go on the air anyway? If you choose the latter, always try to have someone waiting in the wings who won't mind being your last-minute guest.
- **Create a list of people to have as your program guests.** Develop a database of contacts and a schedule of guest appearances. Provide any assistance they may need. Follow through with thank-you notes. If the interview is very successful, bring back the guest for another interview.
- **Monetize your interview.** Make a recording that can be an encore program online. Introduce listeners to follow-up information. Take interview excerpts for inclusion in a print or media presentation featuring several guests discussing a theme or topic.
- **Bring out the best in your guest.** It takes time and practice. Listen to the hosts who do it well, and then develop your own style. And, by all means, enjoy what you do! Unleash the lion in you and the lion you interview.

CHAPTER 5

Go International

In their glory days, lions could be found all over Africa and in parts of Asia and Europe. They roamed the jungles and the plains and do so today. They move among other animals, small and large, to find food, protect their pride, and survive threats of various kinds.

Lions are large animals. Male lions have manes that help them in fighting and protecting their pride. Female lions lack manes and are agile and adept at hunting. The lion's guttural and loud roar can be heard from a distance. The reputation of authority and strength has led to the lion being called the "king of the jungle" and to be a symbol of courage.

Courageous leadership in the international arena is identified with the lion symbol. Examples include political leaders such as Prime Minister Winston Churchill, whose words and witness led England during World War II to join with the Allies to overcome the invasions of Nazi Germany. William Manchester and Paul Reid chronicle the life and times of this courageous leader in *The Last Lion: Winston Spencer Churchill*, a trilogy of biographies covering his enduring legacy.

A second example is the country of Finland, which chose the lion emblem for its national flag and identity. Its history records heroic attempts to achieve and preserve its freedom in the modern era as well as contemporary missions to be a peacekeeper in international disputes.

A third example is Lions Club International. This worldwide service organization consists of 1.35 million members in forty-five thousand clubs in over two hundred countries and geographic areas, making it one of the world's largest volunteer service organizations. The Lions state, "You became a Lion to give something back to your community through direct action. It is the job of Lions Clubs International to help you do that and do it in the most effective way possible. The opportunities for personal and leadership development are evident in activities such as blindness prevention and sight restoration, youth programs and services for children, disaster preparedness and relief, community and environment development."[9]

These and many other opportunities encourage people to have an international outlook and a global perspective in their vocation and volunteer service commitments.

You Cover the World

Name the places in the world where you have lived, studied, worked, or visited.

This chapter explores international perspectives in leadership education and public service, and it begins with several family opportunities. In 1984 my new position in Washington was executive director of the Lutheran Educational Conference of North America (LECNA), an organization of Lutheran colleges and universities in the United States and Canada. Founded in 1910 by college presidents representing the major Lutheran denominations, it developed and maintained the traditions of collegiality, advocacy for causes to benefit Lutheran higher education, and creative projects for member institutions. This job relocation took me from the center of campus life to the edges and interfaces of the denomination, private and public education, and national and international organizations.

Our move to the Washington area brought adaptation and adventures. In the summer of 1984, we went hunting for a place to live, a place to work for Judy, and schools for the girls. Judy landed a teaching position in special education at Rocky Run Intermediate School in Chantilly, Virginia, north of Fairfax and south of Herndon. Hiring procedures in the Fairfax County Schools required sending an application to a central office and waiting to be called for an interview. However, our family went with Judy to several community schools, where she hand-delivered her résumé and met directly with school principals. Her courage, her credentials as a teacher, and her creativity enabled her to gain the special education position. Over the next few years, she developed as a professional to qualify as a master teacher and to become head of her department had we remained in Herndon.

Anne and Marji were students at Chantilly High School, and Sara went to the elementary school nearby. This was the third school they'd entered in three years (Hickory North Carolina and both Salem and Herndon, Virginia). They were excellent students, active in music and sports, and resilient as we kept our Puotinen pride intact during our many moves.

Our new home in the Franklin Farm subdivision was not quite ready for occupancy. Family togetherness took on a new dimension as we lived in a Holiday Inn room in Manassas for a month before moving into our new home. School began for the girls and Judy, and so did my work.

It was an hour and half commute to my office in Washington. I started driving on the Beltway in my 1971 Karmann Ghia, and the stop-and-go traffic resulted in it needing a brand-new clutch within a month. Shifting to public transportation by bus and metro train each day made my commute challenging. Fellow riders carried their *Washington Post* or other papers and read the news each morning while avoiding bumping into one another. At times I ran up and down escalators to make connections and be on time for meetings.

The LECNA office was in the Lutheran Center on 300 C Street Northwest, near the Labor Building. My new position had a dual title. As director of College and University Services of the Lutheran Council in the USA (LCUSA), I worked in an office with LCUSA executives responsible for church wide services, including Lutheran World Relief, public policy, military chaplaincy, and theological studies. Our main LCUSA administrative offices in New York City provided oversight of our Washington staff and called us to New York for periodic meetings. These meetings included four presidents/bishops of the four major Lutheran churches in North America and the directors of LCUSA programs in New York and Washington. The New York meetings, daily contacts with LCUSA colleagues in Washington, and campus visits to nearly forty Lutheran colleges and universities over four years expanded my worldview and my understanding of ecumenical cooperation and the partnership ministries of several Lutheran church bodies.

In the mid-1980s, Lutherans in North America were changing in several ways. Both LECNA and LCUSA existed to provide information and services for cooperative efforts by several Lutheran church organizations in mission and ministry. The American Lutheran Church (ALC), Lutheran Church in America (LCA), Lutheran Church–Missouri Synod (LC-MS), and Association of Evangelical Lutheran Churches (AELC) were each founded under the common heritage of the Lutheran Reformation during the time of Martin Luther in Germany. These Lutheran church bodies developed as immigrants from Germany, Sweden, Norway, Finland, and other countries settled throughout the United States and established congregations and churches to provide worship experiences, Christian education, and care for members. The organization of Lutheran church life in the United States emerged with many common elements and also diversity in church practices.

In 1910, the Lutheran Educational Conference of North America became an organizational forum for college presidents from all Lutheran groups to meet regularly, exchange information on public policy and college programs, and undertake special projects to benefit students, faculty, and administrators. So I entered an arena in 1984 where Lutheran educational leaders knew how to work together. It was a privilege to get to know and serve these top leaders.

The annual LECNA meeting of college presidents was generally held in Washington at a major hotel, followed by individual visits to congressional members representing member districts. My first meeting was the seventy-fifth anniversary of LECNA in 1985, and its board planned a gala event.[10] We invited all Lutheran congressional representatives and senators to attend and also Supreme Court Chief Justice William Rehnquist. Dr. Gary Quehl, president of the Council of Independent Colleges, was the main speaker; he made the case for independent higher education to our special guests. LECNA members rose to the occasion, giving toasts and affirmations of our LECNA heritage. Dinner was served and enjoyed by all.

Judy and I dined at the table with Chief Justice Rehnquist, his wife, and other LECNA members. We learned that in her younger years, his wife had lived in the Copper Country of Michigan. A member at our table asked Rehnquist what his most interesting and important case was, and he judiciously replied it was the one before him at the present time.

After dessert, most of the legislators excused themselves to leave for other meetings or appointments and did not stay to hear Dr. Quehl. We learned that if you want to unleash your lion, don't wait too long. Bring your lead speaker on early to inform and energize your crowd.

You Develop a Major Event

You and your team organize an event that includes VIP guests and others. What do you do to make it a successful program?

My main mentor in Washington was a Capitol Hill veteran named Howard Holcomb. Formerly the chief admissions officer at Gustavus Adolphus College in Minnesota, he was reputed to know and remember the names of every prospective, current, and former student at the school. In Washington he served as the LECNA executive director for several years and diversified his portfolio by consulting with other educational associations.

Howard was a great coach, critic, and collaborator. The LECNA executive director presented a briefing paper on public policy issues for each LECNA annual meeting. My initial drafts tended to be long, wordy, and academic. Howard told me to keep it to one page with several bullet points for each issue. This simple, straightforward piece would be useful talking points for the college presidents when they met with legislators from their congressional districts. This reminded me of my Wake Forest University MBA finance professor, Jack Ferner, who said a strategic plan or a deal can start with several key points on the back of an envelope.

Howard went unheralded, though appreciated, for many years by colleagues in Washington and LECNA institutions. During my Grand View College presidency, we bestowed an honorary doctorate on him; it was well deserved.

People wonder if their voices can be heard in Washington. During the hearings leading to the Tax Reform Act of 1986, some lobbyists in Gucci shoes walked the hallways and offices of Congress to influence legislators regarding some provisions in the bill. The story circulated that a Roman Catholic Christian Brother traveled by bus from California to meet with his legislator about the tax proposals. Face-to-face he presented his case about a proposed revision in the tax code that would drastically impact the financial condition of his organization. The legislator helped change the provision to create a better outcome for religious orders and others in similar circumstances. Advocacy is needed; your voice must be heard.

You Advocate for Worthy Causes

Share an experience when you advocated a worthy cause to your legislator in person or by e-mail, letter, or phone.

My major LECNA responsibilities were event planning for the annual meeting of Lutheran presidents, assisting in public policy advocacy with legislators, and directing several projects. The LECNA office and executive were based then in Washington to be a set of eyes and ears for LECNA members concerning pending legislation that related to higher education. Working with LECNA presidents and our consultant, Howard, we monitored such issues as federal student financial aid and federal tax policies on charitable giving. Attending legislative hearings on these issues, participating in weekly informational briefings by leaders of the American Council of Education and the National Association of Independent Colleges and Universities, and being present for their annual meetings provided me insights on issues and contacts with educational leaders.

- The LECNA projects included thirty-five Lutheran College Nights at regional sites around the country, where college admissions officers recruited prospective students. Howard coordinated this effort and attended every event.
- The LECNA Curriculum Consultation Project, led by Dr. Tom Langevin, sent teams of faculty members from sister colleges to assist the host college faculty in its educational program evaluation and development.
- The LECNA History Project recruited Dr. Richard Solberg to write a published history entitled *Lutheran Higher Education in North America*, which provides historical profiles of LECNA member institutions.
- The LECNA Media Project worked with a media consultant to produce a video depicting campus life at various Lutheran colleges, with narration by TV personality Dick Enberg.
- The LECNA Presidential Partnership Project matched a new incoming Lutheran college president with an experienced president for mentoring, exchange visits to campuses, and assistance in specific areas, such as strategic planning.
- The LECNA International Education Project sent LECNA presidents, spouses, and faculty abroad on short-term study and consultation experiences with educators and church leaders in Africa, Central America, East and West Germany, and the People's Republic of China.

During my four-year term as LECNA executive director, I met three or four times annually with the LECNA board of directors regarding projects and the annual meeting, and I wrote grant proposals to fund the projects noted above. The overall LECNA experience deepened my experience of leadership through partnership and expanded my outreach through national and international contacts and travel.[11]

You Look for Funds

Brainstorm with others on how to find funds for an important task or project by your family, business, or organization.

In the 1980s, the Lutheran church in North America underwent major organizational changes. After years of planning, discussion, and discernment, a new church organization was created to merge into one household these three major groups of Lutherans: the Lutheran Church in America (LCA), the American Lutheran Church in America (ALC), and the Association of Evangelical Lutheran Churches (AELC). The last named smaller group was an offshoot of the Lutheran Church–Missouri Synod (LC-MS), which opted not to enter the new merger because of certain differences of belief in theology and church practices. The story of how this merger took place is too extensive to tell here.

The constituting assembly of the new Evangelical Lutheran Church in America (ELCA) took place in Columbus, Ohio, in 1988. Delegates at this historic meeting approved the key organizational elements of the new church and elected as the new presiding bishop of the ELCA the Rev. Herbert W. Chilstrom. He has written a book describing his experiences in the formative years of the ELCA, entitled *A Journey of Grace: The Formation of a Leader and a Church.*

New beginnings often bring major changes. In preparation for organizing the new ELCA, the four participating Lutheran church bodies in the Lutheran Council in the United States decided to disband LCUSA as an organization and to continue its ministries in other forms. This decision terminated the LCUSA College and University Services office and its executive director position that was one of my titles with assigned duties. Fortunately for LECNA, it continued as a stand-alone organization, maintained its existing programs and projects, and retained my office and other title as LECNA executive director. The LECNA's two full-time staff in Washington also included our capable administrative assistant, Phyllis Harvey. The member Lutheran colleges and universities agreed to continue funding for the LECNA office and staff in Washington.

In January 1988, the LECNA annual meeting was held in Washington and featured the LECNA International Education Project. Former US commissioner of education Ernest Boyer spoke eloquently. Ambassadors or their representatives from fourteen countries came to the meeting, many of them from countries that the LECNA study teams would visit the following summer. Their presence especially excited the LECNA members participating in the study-abroad teams. They looked forward to an introduction to new international connections with educational and church representatives and the exploration of faculty and student exchange agreements. Teams going to Africa, Central America, the People's Republic of China, East and West Germany, and Soviet Union introduced themselves to international representatives.

In 1988 the study tour team to East and West Germany and the Soviet Union included Thiel College president Louis Almen, Luther College president H. George and his wife Jutta Anderson, Roanoke College president Norm and his wife Jo Fintel, Judy and me, and two faculty members from Wittenberg University. Our study group leader was Professor Charles Chatfield, whose teaching expertise in European history and study/travel-abroad experiences with college students equipped him to be our guide. Lou Almen's contacts with Hans Mai of the Evangelical Academy movement in Germany enabled us to have home visits with families, to study current situations involving church and culture, and to experience several historic moments.

We crossed from West Berlin to East Berlin at a checkpoint by the Berlin Wall. Our morning meeting with academics at the Cosmos Club resulted in extensive dialogue with Marxist philosophers. Our afternoon meeting with several seminary students and their professors gave us a glimpse of their challenges to be the church and do ministry. When asked if the Berlin Wall would ever come down, they simply replied, "It will not happen in our lifetime."

Then our study team traveled by bus to several locations in Germany familiar to Lutherans worldwide. We visited Martin Luther's home, where he and his wife, Kathryn, raised their family in the 1500s and regularly hosted university students for meals and table talks. Entering the Wittenberg church where Luther preached, one could imagine seeing and hearing this lion of the Lord, whose words roared in his writings, launching the Protestant Reformation. We stopped briefly at the Wartburg castle, where Luther translated the Bible into the German language after being kidnapped and placed there into safekeeping by his friends. His courageous "Here I Stand" defense of his writings at the Diet of Worms resulted in his life being at risk.

Our study team traveled to Dresden, which still showed the results of being bombed during World War II, and on to several towns where the Evangelical Academy leaders briefed us on the life and work of Christians in their cultural setting. Judy and I made a home visit with a couple whose family of four children discovered a new view of Americans than the ones they saw in TV westerns and dramas. Cultural exchange visits are small but important steps in building knowledge and understanding among people.

Then our study team traveled to the Soviet Union to Moscow for meetings with university professors to talk about cultural exchanges, educational programs, and cooperative projects. Our study team toured many historic sights, and several experiences stand out. Simultaneously the historic Communist Party Congress was underway in Moscow, eclipsing our academic conversations. President Mikhail Gorbachev was boldly stating his vision for glasnost and perestroika to those assembled.

Our guides took us later to a Christian monastery in Zagorsk— around forty-six miles from Moscow—for another historic moment. Those gathered there were launching a yearlong celebration of the thousandth anniversary of the Russian Orthodox Church. Metropolitan Filaret, a senior church official, said, "The Russian Orthodox Church blesses wholeheartedly the good developments in this country and calls on its flock to take an active part in the process of restructuring." In conversations with local church leaders, they described their struggles and perseverance during the Soviet era, and those gathered for earnest prayer made a lasting impression.

This historical background helped us to better understand the tour guide's commentary later in Moscow. She pointed out several sites, saying, "This is no longer a functioning church but a cultural museum." Through these brief encounters and other indications, we were impressed with this a country whose landmarks included centuries-old Christianity, current Communist control, and the creative beginnings of democratization.

Our air travel and stay in Saint Petersburg (Leningrad) included visiting the Hermitage Museum and learning the history of Stalingrad and the extensive loss of life during World War II battles. At the end of the day, our study team celebrated the wedding anniversary of two members and shared stories of our adventures together during the past week. Our thoughts also turned to the other LECNA study teams, which went to Central America, Nigeria, and the People's Republic of China. We finally flew to Helsinki, Finland, as the last leg of our trip together. It had been a memorable and enjoyable learning experience, and we bid each other a fond farewell.

> ### *You Explore New Regions*
>
> Take a moment to choose an international location to visit, and then read about it, watch videos, talk to those who know it firsthand, and travel there when time and resources permit.

Thereafter Judy and I traveled by plane to Dusseldorf, Germany, to reunite with our family. Earlier, in mid-June, Judy, Marji, Sara, and I had traveled by plane to Germany. The girls were met by Judy's sister Pat McKenna, her husband Kevin McKenna, and their children, Katie and Sean, for several weeks in Dusseldorf. Their family lived there for several years while Kevin completed a work assignment for 3M, headquartered in Minneapolis–Saint Paul. With our daughters in good hands, we were able to connect with our LECNA study team members for our trip together.

The McKenna's took our family of four on several day trips around the region. On one occasion, Pat and Kevin drove us to Mettlach, Germany, and the Villeroy & Boch Outlet Center, which featured attractive porcelain, glass, crystal, cutlery, gift items, and accessories. There I fulfilled the promise made on our marriage engagement day in February 29, 1964, as now Judy joyfully made her selections. Pat and Kevin delivered the carefully boxed treasures to Judy several months later, when they returned to the United States for Kevin to begin a new assignment for 3M.

My final LECNA International Education task involved working with a group of LECNA study travelers to organize a debriefing conference at Carthage College in Wisconsin in August 1988. Many participants in the four LECNA trips returned with exciting stories of experiences, contacts with overseas educational and church organizations, and with information to share with their home campuses.

All LECNA members received the conference written report with findings and suggestions. We recognized that international education in various forms already existed in their institutions, so the ideas and information could enhance existing efforts. LECNA trip participants also pledged themselves to encourage and support international education experiences for their students, faculty, administrators, and alumni.

Suggestions for Going International with Educational or Business Groups

- **Identify places and people to pursue in your global vision.** LECNA served more than forty Lutheran colleges and universities throughout North America, and LECNA went global with the International Education Project.
- **Choose the best route of entry for your business.** LECNA identified four world regions for study, exploration, and potential partnerships with educational organizations and carefully planned project activities as part of its global vision.
- **Use government help and find relevant support organizations.** LECNA contacted US congressional members from LECNA member districts, Office of Education grant offices, selected international embassies, and church groups.
- **Take part in a trade mission.** LECNA members assembled in four study teams that completed fact-finding, networking, and project development in Central America, Eastern and Western Europe, Peoples Republic of China, and West Africa
- **Monitor operations.** Each study team included a team leader with educational expertise in the region. This leader designed the trip, made contacts with local leaders, briefed team members, and monitored all activities during the trip.

- **Follow the rules of etiquette.** Before the study trips, all team members were briefed on local customs and traditions. Regional contacts gave more specific information on people and places being visited. While on tour LECNA team members held daily debriefing sessions about their experiences.

- **Market your business internationally.** Face-to-face meetings with international hosts allowed us to exchange contact information, explore educational agreements, and have student and faculty exchanges. After their trip, LECNA members went home to work on international education projects on their own campus.

- **Learn from others' experiences.** Three kinds of learning occurred for LECNA members: immersion in another country's culture and people; information exchange in daily contacts with hosts and team members; and the implementation of ideas, exchange agreements, and projects.

CHAPTER 6

Connect with Constituents

Lion cubs learn to live and lead from older lions in many ways. As a prelude to the rigors of hunting, mating, and defending against predators, cub playtime is essential and beneficial. It allows cubs to develop their strengths and habits. "The playfield is a schoolroom where young cubs learn cunningness and improve their skill and creativity ... The games cubs play reflect the society in which they lives, as they mime the gestures and behavior of their parents ... Older cubs within a pride will never use all their strength against a weaker companion. That is how they learn to play together. Also, by reducing his own chances of winning, the individual with the upper hand also prolongs the pleasure of the play."[12]

So you are or want to be an organizational leader. How do you get to this position? What life experiences help you to serve and succeed? Our playing field has many locations at home, school, work, and elsewhere. Learning to play the game together with other leaders in these venues makes life enjoyable and worthwhile.

During an annual LECNA meeting of Lutheran college and university presidents in Washington, DC, one leader said, "The presidents here today vary by age, gender, education, professional experience, aptitude, appearance, and other attributes. Another important variable is aspiration. Some presidents may have worked a long time for the position they desired; others develop a willingness to serve in that role based on their career achievements, encouragement by others, opportunity, and other situational factors. There are many pathways to the leadership position that you desire."

Each person's pathway to a top leadership position has numerous stepping-stones. You have to walk the walk and talk the talk to reach your desired position. Here are key points in my journey in 1987–88 to become the next president of Grand View College in Des Moines.

1. A LECNA presidential colleague sent a letter nominating me for the advertised presidential opening at Grand View College.
2. The Presidential Search Committee received my application letter and résumé of educational achievements and leadership service.
3. My candidacy advanced to a first round of interviews off campus with selected applicants in January 1988.
4. I was chosen as one of three finalists, and I went with Judy to the Grand View campus for interviews with college constituents, such as students, faculty, administrators, staff, trustees, alumni, and community leaders.
5. During the LECNA Annual Meeting in early February 1988, the Grand View board chairman phoned me to say that the Presidential Search Committee wanted to recommend me as their presidential nominee. He reviewed terms of the proposed contract, and I agreed to meet with members of the board soon.
6. In early spring, the Grand View College board of trustees welcomed Judy and me at a get acquainted luncheon. Then in meeting assembled they elected me to be their next president and to follow in the footsteps of two Grand View presidents with long and productive tenures.

Dr. Ernest Nielsen, a native of Denmark and a University of Chicago PhD, ably represented the Danish folk school tradition championed in Denmark by N. F. S. Grundtvig. Nielsen developed a strong liberal arts and career education that resulted in the college being fully accredited as a two-year college by the North Central Association of Colleges and Schools. He continued to reside in the Des Moines area and attend various college events.

His successor, Rev. Karl Langrock, had a strong stewardship and fundraising background and led the transition of Grand View from a two-year to a four-year college, with business, education, and nursing being the lead programs. Langrock was a LECNA member president, and he gave me valuable information and insight to begin my presidential tenure. My challenge was to build on the strong foundation laid by others who preceded me. (See Thorvald Hansen's *That All Good Seed Strike Root: A Centennial History of Grand View College* for an informative history of the school, including my presidential years.)

You Share Your Vision

What would you do in your new leadership position? Briefly state your vision for your organization.

Before we moved from Herndon to Des Moines in August of 1988 so I could begin my dream job, a *Des Moines Register* reporter phoned me. Following her congratulatory words, she asked me to share my vision for Grand View College. Situated a mile north of the state capital building, the college offered its educational programs to students of varying educational and economic backgrounds. A marketing slogan on a city bus read, "Shape Your Future at Grand View" to attract first-time and transfer students to enroll for courses. Faculty members prided themselves in teaching and mentoring students. Tuition and fees were the lowest among the over twenty-eight four-year private colleges in Iowa to enable promising students to attend and succeed.

The brand that Grand View had built over the years was clear and dear to me. My vision was to build on and enhance Grand View's reputation as a 4-A institution. Its bond with constituents and community had a 4-A value. My purpose in leadership would be to emphasize accessibility, affordability, activities, and achievement for the students of Grand View College:

- Accessibility for students who desired to learn
- Affordability for families who needed financial assistance
- Curricular and cocurricular activities for students who sought a well-rounded life
- Achievement and progress toward graduation and a rewarding career

When a new president arrives on campus, there are many things to do and people to see. A key to survival, success, and significance is a life and work style where you connect with constituents. You greet them on campus, and you go into the larger community. In earlier times, a general guideline held that presidents should spend 50 percent of their time on campus and 50 percent off campus. Today the off-campus percentage is greater, especially during major funding campaigns. Early on, I began telling colleagues and friends that a GOTO key is essential on one's computer *and* in connecting with constituents. "Get Out of The Office." Meet with people who need you and you need. Talk with friends and critics alike.

My formal installation as president was a festive occasion for the college, community, and my family. The ceremony featured greetings from representatives of our students and alumni, faculty and staff, trustees and representatives from other colleges, the Evangelical

Lutheran Church in America, and the regional community. My parents were unable to attend, but Judy's parents did.

During my installation service at St. John's Lutheran Church in Des Moines, Judy read a scriptural lesson. My graduate school mentor, Dr. Martin Marty of the University of Chicago Divinity School, gave the main address. My remarks highlighted the achievement of a long-held dream to be a college president, the acknowledgement of many people that made that day possible, and an affirmation to work with all constituents in shaping the future at Grand View College.

Grand View Board Chairman Robert Hudson emceed the event and joined with Rev. Lowell Almen, secretary of the Evangelical Lutheran Church in America, to install me formally as president. Our daughters Anne, Marji, and Sara came forward to place the presidential medallion around my neck and give me a group hug. It was a joyous moment, and a festive meal followed the ceremony.

A videotape of the ceremony shows various participants at the installation event. This chapter details several examples of connections I made with these constituents.

Students. During the first week of classes, the new student-body president, Michelle Wilkinson, introduced herself, and we decided that we should visit various classes to meet the students. An experienced faculty member welcomed us to his classroom with these words: "Students, I would like to introduce the newest and most important president on our campus … Michelle Wilkinson." She spoke briefly and then I remarked, "Yes, students come first at Grand View, and faculty are second. Our job in administration is to help you all succeed."

It was important to meet with student groups, lunch with them, and attend their academic events and ball games. A presidential colleague once began his tenure by spending several weeks as a dormitory resident before his family moved to town to be with him. My variation on the theme was "a president in residence for the weekend." In my short stay in the residence hall, I glimpsed what goes on in student life, shot some hoops with basketball team members, and listened about living in a dormitory.

My greatest satisfaction was seeing students' progress and achievement in earning associate's and baccalaureate degrees in their major fields of study at Grand View College. At school opening in the fall, I welcomed incoming students and parents, and in the spring I presided at commencements as proud graduating students and their family members gathered to celebrate their academic success.

Some graduates enrolled at the college right after high school; others were adult learners that returned to complete their studies or came to begin a new career. By seeking to be a school for life and valuing the potential in each student, Grand View College became for many students their pool of discovery of their talents and opportunities to succeed and serve. "Unleash the Lion in You" was a theme made real in the lives of many students.

A single parent named Diane spoke briefly at a noon meeting of the Des Moines Rotary Club about her life and Grand View College experiences:

> I am divorced, a single mother of two children, and a recovering alcoholic. I woke up one morning and looked into the mirror and realized that there has to be more in me than what I see. So I went back to high school and completed the GED program. Then I went to Des Moines Area Community College and earned an associate's degree. Thereafter Grand View offered me a scholarship to complete my four-year degree in human services. Along the way I did

73

an internship with our dean of students and organized a food drive for needy families and a Halloween party for the local kids. In a few weeks I will graduate from Grand View as an honor student and then in the fall begin a master's degree program at Drake University. My goal is to get a leadership position in social services, stay in the Des Moines area, and give back to the community that helped me get my life back on track. I can help others do the same.

All assembled heard a promising community leader roar with courage and strength. She had unleashed her lion.

Faculty. Those who teach and serve at church-related colleges are talented in many ways, dedicated to their students and profession, and noteworthy for their various achievements. For example, Dr. Douglas Larche served as a professor of theater arts and speech at several colleges and universities, including Grand View. His achievements include being a Fulbright scholar, many published books and plays, international university teaching and research, and being adviser and director of cultural programming for Iowa and its governor, Tom Vilsack.

Larche demonstrated a willingness to disrupt traditional thinking and approaches. To complement the children's Mother Goose stories, he wrote *Father Gander,* a variation of nursery rhymes, and told some of them on the *Tonight Show Starring Johnny Carson.* He wrote the scripts, composed the songs, and directed the productions of several plays dealing with contemporary social issues. His *Angels in the Snow* depicted church and governmental leaders in Germany facing situations before and after the removal of the Berlin Wall. His play on Sojourner Truth views her courage in civil rights leadership as the backdrop for justice issues in a contemporary academic situation.

Larche's students appreciate his willingness to give them opportunities to perform and succeed. He encourages and helps academically and physically challenged students to realize their potential. And his director notes before and after each performance provide valuable coaching and suggestions for how to make it better next time.

Administration. Every president needs a team, and I expressed my willingness to work with the current administrative officers. Nonetheless, transitions occurred during my eight years, with some officers retiring and others moving on. The selection of worthy and valued replacements required search processes similar to my own. Leadership team colleagues served in vice presidential positions, such as academic affairs, financial affairs, development, and public relations, and in director positions, such as admissions, student affairs, and college chaplain. In turn, they had faculty, administrative staff, and support staff reporting to them. Their commitment, expertise, and creativity were critical to our leadership team efforts during the growth of the college and when overcoming the Flood of 1993 (to be described in a later chapter).

Trustees. Transition became a new tradition in the selection of the chairman of the board of trustees. During Karl Langrock's presidency, a board chair generally served a long term. Prior to my arrival, the board of trustees agreed to establish a new pattern of a two-year term for the chairman on a nonrecurring basis. During my eight years at Grand View, six different board chairs served in that position. It was the board's decision to favor change over continuity, and the close working relationship of the college president and the board chair became very important to develop and maintain.

The Grand View board of trustees consisted of alumni, church, and community representatives along with educational leaders and friends. The mayor of Des Moines was a board member, and he came to my office during my first week at Grand View and said to me, "Mr. President, we want you to get out of the dugout [my office] and get on the playing field."

Community. Responding to that challenge, I helped local citizens create the Union Park Neighborhood Association—a citizens' organization that met regularly about local housing, city services, and other community needs.[13] My community involvements also included belonging to the Des Moines Rotary Club and serving on the board of directors of both the Iowa Lutheran Hospital and the Iowa Ballet.

Educational organizations. My membership in the Iowa Association of Colleges and Universities meant attending quarterly meetings with the presidents of the three major public universities, the various community colleges in Iowa, and twenty-nine independent colleges. Our work involved reviewing and approving any new academic programs to be initiated by individual colleges and universities. All member presidents also belonged to the Iowa College Foundation. It organized various presidents into teams of three to four people and assigned them to various regions of Iowa to meet with area businesses and solicit financial gifts for ICF institutions. This opportunity brought me to several rural communities and many Iowa residents shared a strong commitment to education.

Government. Iowa independent college presidents worked together to develop good relations with legislators from their areas and Governor Terry Branstad. Their strong support of the Iowa Tuition Grant program enabled many independent Iowa college students to receive this financial aid for their studies. Governor Branstad came to the Grand View campus to make presentations, attend cultural and sporting events, and connect with the Danish traditions of our school.

In like manner, it was important to be in contact with the Iowa legislators in the US Congress. Senator Tom Harkins and Representative Neil Davis were ranking members of congressional committees involved with education and appropriations. My conversations with them covered federal student aid legislation, such as Pell Grant appropriations, and educational program grant requests for Grand View College programs. These much-needed financial resources helped students to achieve their educational and career goals.

Intercollegiate athletics. Grand View's baseball, basketball, softball, and volleyball teams competed in the National Association of Intercollegiate Athletics. In May 1991, the baseball team made it to the NAIA World Series in Idaho for a third time and successfully bid on having Des Moines as the designated NAIA World Series site for the next three years. During the fall of 1991, Coach Lou Yacinich mobilized college and community volunteers to develop and promote the 1992 NAIA World Series events with help from NAIA officials, local organizations, and the media. With continued cooperation, support, and leadership, Grand View College, Sec Taylor Stadium, and Des Moines hosted the NAIA World Series for two more years in 1993 and 1994.

After my presidency, Grand View University significantly increased its athletic facilities and sports program over a decade to include twenty-four sports for men and women. In 2012, 2013, and 2014, the Vikings won the NAIA national championship in wrestling. In 2013, the Vikings won the NAIA national championship in football.

You Go to Bat for a Worthy Cause

Remember when you were asked to support an important project or person in jeopardy, and note what action you took.

Church. It was exciting to throw out the ceremonial first pitch at one of the NAIA World Series games in 1992, but it was a season to go to bat for Grand View College on another playing field. Founded in 1988, the Evangelical Lutheran Church in America was facing a financial crisis. Presiding Bishop Herbert Chilstrom and the ELCA Church Council considered various cost reduction strategies, including reducing or eliminating ELCA funding for its twenty-nine colleges.

Presidents of ELCA colleges advocated for our institutions. My letter to Bishop Chilstrom outlined Grand View College's partnership with the ELCA in developing future leaders for church and society; and my plea also enumerated ten different ways and programs that Grand View offered to fulfill that mission. In asking for continued ELCA financial support for our college, my final statement said, "Trustees, faculty, and staff leaders at Grand View are excited and engaged in significant ministry. We have much to offer the church. Our best is yet to be. It is not the right time to cut off the ELCA investment in Grand View and other colleges. Wise stewardship calls for taking care of these treasures of the ELCA and enabling them to return the church's investment a hundred fold."

In his autobiography, *A Journey of Grace*, Bishop Chilstrom recalled his meeting in Chicago with a dozen or so ELCA college presidents.[14] He reminded our representatives that ELCA congregations were accessible to the colleges for recruiting students and receiving wills and bequests from members. Further he urged the colleges to redouble their fundraising efforts among their graduates and friends. During a time when many interest groups within the ELCA were directly advocating that Bishop Chilstrom maintain financial support for their programs, evidently his session with the college presidents was very challenging. He noted, "All in all, it was a most difficult session." Nonetheless, he demonstrated in his achievements in eight years as ELCA's presiding bishop a remarkable record of accomplishments, strength of spirit, and courage—grace under pressure.

Church connections at Grand View occurred in other ways. A full-time college chaplain conducted worship each week, counseled students, and taught part-time in a religion department with several faculty members. Two ELCA congregations (Grand View Lutheran and Luther Memorial Lutheran) were situated on and by the campus. Reports of Grand View's programs were sent and orally communicated at the three ELCA synods in Iowa.

Alumni. Two-year and four-year graduates of Grand View advanced in their various career fields and lived in many US and international communities. The annual homecoming reunions, known as Studenterfest, welcomed them to several days of food and fellowship, folk dancing and presentations, award ceremonies and worship experiences. Several alumni came from as far away as California, Washington, and Oregon.

Crises on campus. In colleges, most students experience successes and setbacks in courses they take, relationships they have, and other situations. My prior experiences as a college dean introduced me to scores of students going through such learning and growth processes. These events, however, lacked the gravity of three tragic events during my first few months at Grand View.

First, the son of a faculty member committed suicide. Second, two students driving home for Thanksgiving were crushed to death by an oncoming freight train at a railroad track crossing.

> ### *You Care for Others*
>
> Share a time that you responded to a tragedy in the life of colleague, client, or family member.

The third unexpected event received major media coverage. The *Des Moines Register* ran a series of five stories of the incident, which occurred on November 19, 1988. [15]

Grand View College was the site for a state real-estate licensing exam that Saturday morning. A nearby community resident came to campus early that morning to take the exam. As she sat in her car in the college parking lot, reviewing her notes before going in, the car door suddenly opened. An assailant overpowered her, drove away from campus, and then robbed and raped her. After he threatened her with further harm if she went to the police, he left her alone. She went to a nearby hospital for medical treatment and reported the attack to the police. The rest of the Pulitzer Prize–winning news series detailed how this married mother of three children identified the assailant from police photographs and participated in the public trial that brought him to justice. Subsequently a television documentary dramatized her courageous effort to take back her life and career.

The Grand View campus community was shocked and concerned over this event. Our administration reviewed and strengthened security measures. More outdoor campus lighting of parking lots and walkways were added. Students received information on self-protection steps they could take.

The lessons learned from this incident and the two student deaths were the importance of reaching out to families and other survivors, improving safety and security for those you serve, and standing with those needing support as they seek to rebuild their lives.

Presidential priorities. Colleges, like all organizations, require teamwork, systems, and orderly processes on a daily basis to take care of business, students, faculty, and learning opportunities. What can a president or any other leader do to make this process flow smoothly? Luther College president H. George Anderson remarked to me that his leadership involved steering a ship when up-and-down movement on one side of the boat by excited passengers would result in movement by people on the other side of the boat to keep it steady and on course.

He applied this wisdom in the coaching that he provided to me. Leadership involves charting the course and keeping on it. Over coffee one day, he asked what we were doing at Grand View College at the time. My response included a lengthy list of various programs and activities. Then he asked for my top three priorities. After some reflection, I gave him three, believing they would suffice. But Anderson asked, "Can you give it to me in one sentence? What is the focus of your vision, work, and activities?" My response was that further reflection was needed.

> *You Focus on Priorities*
>
> Share your top three priorities in life and work today. Then summarize them in one sentence.

A legacy from my dad. My one sentence came after a life-changing experience. In the spring of 1992, my father, Kully, entered his final stage of life at Luther Park Health Center near Grand View College. In his room one evening, he reminisced about people he cared for and things he did. On his bed stand was a daily calendar with a Bible verse for each day. The verse from Isaiah 4:3–4 for June 22 read, "The voice of him that cries in the wilderness, prepare you the way of the LORD, make straight in the desert a highway for our God. Every valley shall be exalted, and every mountain and hill shall be made low: and the crooked shall be made straight and the rough places plain."

Connecting the ancient text to my father's life and legacy in that moment gave me new insight and inspiration. Kully tried and often succeeded in making things better for his family and his community. His taking care of the family farm and his parents, advocating for a new highway and other improvements, and other leadership activities flashed through my mind. He was handing his legacy over to me.

Kully passed away that night, giving me the inspiration for the one sentence that became my mantra for the forthcoming academic year at Grand View: "We can make it better." A few weeks later, in my annual speech to faculty and staff colleagues to begin a new academic year, I included this challenge: "In whatever we say and do, let us think creatively, act decisively, and continue courageously as a learning community. We can make it better!" My dad had not attended my installation festivities in the fall of 1988, yet he came later to live near Grand View and to leave his mark on my presidency.

Suggestions for Becoming an Effective Leader

- **Keep your word.** Don't make promises you can't keep; make those you can keep.
- **Be fair to all.** A good leader shows no favorites. Don't allow friendships to keep you from being fair to all members of your team or group.

- **Be a good communicator.** You don't need a commanding voice to be a good leader, but you must be willing to step out front with an effective "Let's go." A good leader knows how to give and receive information so that everyone understands what's going on.

- **Be flexible.** Everything doesn't always go as planned. Be prepared to shift to plan B when plan A doesn't work.

- **Be organized.** The time you spend planning will be repaid many times over. Keep records of people who agree to help, and expect them to be responsible.

- **Delegate.** Some leaders assume that the job will not get done unless they do it themselves. Most people like to be challenged with a task. Empower your team to do things they have never tried.

- **Set an example.** The most important thing you can do is lead by example. Whatever you do, others are likely to do the same. A cheerful attitude can keep everyone's spirits up.

- **Give praise.** The best way to get credit is to give it away. Recognition takes many forms: personal notes, public affirmations, promotions, and salary increases.

- **Ask for help.** You have many resources at your disposal. When confronted with a situation you don't know how to handle, ask someone with more experience for advice and direction.

CHAPTER 7

Get and Give a Million

Lions do most of their hunting at night, and they often hunt as a team. Doing it together allows them to hunt bigger prey than a solitary cat can. Lionesses do between 80 to 90 percent of their hunting within a pride. They form hunting groups especially when they attack difficult and larger prey. Solitary hunting by both males and females also takes place to maintain the food supply for their pride. Hunting and gathering are essential habits for lions and other animals too.

Humans "hunt" for the food and other resources that we need through regular work and individual effort. Income is needed to feed a family, to grow a business, and to support public and private organizations. Leaders seek funding from a variety of sources, such as fees, payment for services, government subsidies, foundation grants, corporate donations, and personal gifts. Solitary hunting sometimes succeeds, yet a team approach to revenue generation often leads to significant results.

You Hunt for Funds

Take a moment to note the different types of income and revenue needed and used by your family and your organization.

Leaders are required to look for more funds, so this chapter details a way to get and give $1 million. During my high school years, my favorite TV programs featured baseball, basketball, and football. Nonetheless, a program with stories about people who received instant wealth through a gift from a very generous benefactor sparked my interest and imagination.

The Millionaire was an American anthology series that aired on CBS from January 19, 1955, to June 8, 1960. It explored the ways sudden and unexpected wealth changed the lives of recipients for better or for worse, and it became a five-season hit. It told the stories of people who were given $1 million from a benefactor who insisted they never know him. The benefactor was John Beresford Tipton Jr. TV viewers heard his voice making observations and giving instructions. They also saw only his arm as he extended a cashier's check for $1 million each week to his executive secretary, Michael Anthony. It became Anthony's job to deliver that check to its intended, unsuspecting recipient.

The resulting weekly drama affirmed the abundance of the benefactor and depicted how the recipients used their time, talent, and newly received treasure to change their life in constructive or destructive ways.

The Millionaire offered a fantasy for viewers as they imagined a knock on the door and an announcement of $1 million check for them to use in any way. I wondered how I could obtain such a sum, and how it should be spent and/or invested. This popular program raised the topic of good stewardship of whatever amount of money and wealth we might acquire and use.

Jesus of Nazareth taught often about money; eleven of his thirty-nine parables included it. One of every seven verses in the Gospel of

Luke refers to money. In his parable on the talents, Jesus told a story about how to get and spend money wisely.

> "Again, it will be like a man going on a journey, who called his servants and entrusted his wealth to them. To one he gave five bags of gold, to another two bags, and to another one bag, each according to his ability. Then he went on his journey. The man who had received five bags of gold went at once and put his money to work and gained five bags more. So also, the one with two bags of gold gained two more. But the man who had received one bag went off, dug a hole in the ground and hid his master's money.

> "After a long time the master of those servants returned and settled accounts with them. The man who had received five bags of gold brought the other five. 'Master,' he said, 'you entrusted me with five bags of gold. See, I have gained five more.'

> "His master replied, 'Well done, good and faithful servant! You have been faithful with a few things; I will put you in charge of many things. Come and share your master's happiness!'

> "The man with two bags of gold also came. 'Master,' he said, 'you entrusted me with two bags of gold; see, I have gained two more.'

> "His master replied, 'Well done, good and faithful servant! You have been faithful with a few things; I will put you in charge of many things. Come and share your master's happiness!'

"Then the man who had received one bag of gold came. 'Master,' he said, 'I knew that you are a hard man, harvesting where you have not sown and gathering where you have not scattered seed. So I was afraid and went out and hid your gold in the ground. See, here is what belongs to you.'

"His master replied, 'You wicked, lazy servant! So you knew that I harvest where I have not sown and gather where I have not scattered seed? Well then, you should have put my money on deposit with the bankers, so that when I returned I would have received it back with interest.

"So take the bag of gold from him and give it to the one who has ten bags.

"For whoever has will be given more, and they will have abundance. Whoever does not have, even what they have will be taken from them.'" (Matthew 25:14–29)

This matter of money becomes especially crucial when you lack it, which was my case during graduate school. Doing research for my doctoral dissertation required a major decision for my family, as the relevant materials were not available in Chicago, where I served as pastor of Trinity Lutheran Church on Wilson Avenue. It became necessary to resign my position and relocate. Our second daughter, Marji, was born in August of 1970, and one month later our family of four moved to Hancock, Michigan, for my doctoral research in several libraries and archives. We had some savings, and Suomi College provided us lodging and stipends for my part-time work. Economic reality set in like the winter snows in the Copper Country.

In January of 1971, my search for a teaching position resulted in sending application letters and résumés to about two hundred colleges and universities. Most of them said they had no openings, yet one position was available at Central Michigan University. The search team invited me to campus for an interview and offered me that job. In life, we receive many no's, and one yes can turn your life around. So Judy, our daughters, and I moved the next summer to Mount Pleasant, Michigan, to begin a new life together.

My teaching career began the fall of 1971 at Central Michigan University. Drs. Stan Walters, Charles Pfeiffer, and Mathias Zahniser served as the guiding force for a new program in religious studies at CMU. My new portfolio of four courses per term focused on religion in America and contemporary moral issues. It covered a wide range of topics relating to personal morality, social concerns, and global issues, with an emphasis on theory and practice. Rather than writing a typical term paper, students had an opportunity for teamwork, achievement, and sharing resources for the common good.

Like Michael Anthony on *The Millionaire*, I told the students, "Suppose that we as a class receive $1 million. An unknown benefactor is giving us this money as a gift to spend, not on ourselves but on people in our community with many problems and needs. Now it's up to you to divide into small teams that will identify a specific community need of a particular group. Find out more about their situation, and think about a solution to assist them. After your fact finding, write a grant proposal for a portion of the million-dollar gift to be used in your proposed project. Then each team will make an oral presentation to the entire class and turn in your written grant request. We will add up the total amount of funds being sought by everyone and then decide as a group the amount to be awarded each team."

This distributive justice exercise involved moral and practical decisions. The students determined that an equal split for each team would not do. They wanted a competitive process where higher-quality projects would receive the most funding. I taught them ethical theory and grant-writing skills; they taught one another creative thinking, advocacy for worthwhile causes, and good stewardship of available funds.

Several teams identified programs ranging from child care to senior citizen assistance. One team focused on the housing needs of the nearby Native American community. One young man voluntarily spent a weekend in the local jail as a first step to proposing educational assistance and reading materials for prisoners. This homework assignment for students became a lesson for life on how to give something back to the community even as you seek success in your career.

You Spend Money Wisely

Brainstorm with your team on how to spend $1 million wisely to assist a group needing help in your community, region, or elsewhere.

After my return to Suomi College as dean of faculty in 1974, the million-dollar interactive case study became popular in my Ethical Problems course. The setting changed from Central Michigan University, with thirteen thousand undergraduate and graduate students, to Suomi College and its four hundred students. This smaller school in a small town needed an entrepreneurial academic dean that taught two courses each semester, administered faculty and academic programs, and sought federal and state grants for special projects with a team of administrators and faculty. Theory turned to practice, and here are a few creative endeavors.

Upon my arrival in 1974, Suomi College received a grant from the US Office of International Education to start a new two-year program called Three Cultures on a Northland Campus, a grant program funded by the US Office of International Education. Development Director Arnold Lack wrote the grant proposal, presented it to the Office of Education staff in Washington, and received the program grant. Dean of Students Dave Strang and I worked with faculty, students, and others to implement the program.

The three cultures at Suomi College included Finnish American— the heritage of the college founders and many local residents. The second culture was that of the forty Suomi students from the Micronesian Islands in the South Pacific. The former Suomi dean of students, Michael Caldwell, initially recruited them. His father was a Trust Territory administrator in the Micronesian Islands and desired opportunities for Micronesian youth to receive college-level education in the United States. The US government provided student financial aid for Micronesian students, and the Caldwell contacts enabled a partnership to develop and continue. Incoming Micronesian students at Suomi College received orientation, special services, and courses to meet their career objectives. The new Suomi dean of students, Dave Strang, became a dynamic teacher, counselor, and partner in leading the program activities in the Three Cultures on a Northland Campus project.

The third culture of American minorities came from Suomi students and the surrounding community. The Native American Chippewa tribal community had a reservation near Baraga, on the shore of Lake Superior, some thirty miles away from the Suomi College, and a score of tribal students enrolled in classes offered both at our main Hancock campus and at the Baraga tribal center. African American Suomi students numbered around thirty and were recruited from Milwaukee, Detroit, and other urban settings.

The Three Cultures grant called for faculty to develop curricular content in existing courses and to offer cultural enrichment and cross-cultural communication and understanding on campus and in the community. Initial faculty hesitancy turned to receptivity through a curricular innovation. Working with academic departments, we placed regularly scheduled courses on a Monday-Tuesday-Thursday-Friday calendar and created an open Wednesday for a special course during fourteen weeks in the second semester.

Faculty/staff/student task forces in four areas (Finnish, Micronesian, minorities, and contemporary issues) planned and implemented a single course available for credit and for community auditors that featured learning experiences in all four areas. We devoted three to four Wednesdays a semester to activities and events in each theme area. The grant provided national and international speakers, film presentations, meals with cultural foods, and other activities. The Wonderful Wednesday's program received positive responses from students, faculty, townspeople, and the US International Education Office. They also funded the Three Cultures program for a second year, and our emphasis in 1976 focused on the American bicentennial.

My visits to Washington Office of Education Grant Program areas continued, and we received a grant to initiate a new cooperative education program on campus. The grant funded a full-time director to work with Suomi College faculty and staff in curriculum design, student placement, and contacts with employers. Students in such fields as business, human services, and nursing had their course work on campus. They went off campus to field experiences and/ or internships in local business, human services, and health care organizations with mentors in these fields.

Similarly, contacts with Michigan educational agencies in Lansing by Arnold Lack led to grant-funded programs such as HEADS-UP: Health and Heritage Education Adult Delivery System in the Upper Peninsula. It focused on providing educational experiences for older residents in ten different off-campus sites in a one-hundred-mile radius of Hancock. Suomi faculty members received a stipend and travel expenses to provide workshop experiences for seniors at each site. These popular once-a-week lunch-and-learn events on topics of interest to them extended the college outreach to an underserved population. While Head Start area programs served children, HEADS-UP reached older learners. We also recruited a local senior scholar at each site to recruit students and coordinate the local workshop experiences. One of the ten sites was my hometown, Amasa, where my father had served as the senior scholar.

HEADS-UP finished its first year in the summer with a festive Senior-American Day on campus. Participants came from the ten lunch-and-learn sites to enjoy a special luncheon, a senior fashion show, and workshops. We gave awards to the oldest person in several categories, such as teacher, police officer, firefighter, miner, lumber worker, grandfather, and grandmother. The oldest person to receive an award was ninety-five, and it was given on a day where the temperature climbed to ninety-five degrees, a rare occurrence in the Copper Country by Lake Superior.

These grant-funded programs illustrate the opportunities to get money and spend it creatively. Personal contacts with directors of program areas are important—by letter, phone, and visit. Writing a successful grant proposal requires careful reading of the guidelines provided in the Federal Register and by state agencies or private foundations. Successful grants must address specifically the desired elements, the objectives, and the expected results of the program. Sometimes grant administrators make on-site visits to strengthen the relationships of project partners and confirm the values and results of the program.

The project examples cited above amounted to $20,000 to $100,000 a year for each program and indicate that smaller organizations can compete in receiving such funds as well as larger institutions that seek and receive grants in the range of $100,000 to $1 million. Working with campus colleagues as well as individual and organizational investors in implementing various grant projects in the 1970s helped to prepare me for leading a multiyear, multimillion-dollar capital campaign at Grand View College in 1988–96.

You Celebrate Success

Share your significant results in raising funds with your team at home, at work, or with a voluntary organization, and note the top reasons for your success.

An important asset for a leader is a rewarding, wholesome family life. My return in 1974 to Suomi College as its dean of faculty enabled Judy and me to invest in a new ranch-style home in Houghton. Anne and Marji attended Houghton Elementary School and enjoyed playing with neighborhood children as well as taking family excursions in the Copper Country and to grandparents' homes. Our third daughter, Sara Lynn, was born in 1974 and became a lively addition to our household.

Both Judy and I were actively involved in physical fitness programs at the Suomi College Paavo Nurmi Physical Education Center, and all three girls learned to swim in its pool. They also enjoyed swimming in chilly Lake Superior in the summer and sledding in the significant snows that fell. Sports and physical fitness became a lifetime commitment for our family of five and an important element in our weekly regimen.

* * * *

Now we fast-forward to Grand View College to my first months there. Every day is show time for a college president. Show up for work and make good things happen, especially in the area of a major funding campaign. When I first arrived, fundraising consultant Ron

Mulder came to brief me on the progress to date. The case statement for the new campaign was taking shape: capital projects such as a library addition and a new business and computer science academic building, funding for student scholarships and faculty salaries, and additions to the endowment fund. He suggested an overall goal of $5 million for the campaign. In 1988, for a college of the size and history of Grand View, this goal was a major challenge. We surpassed it, and following are the challenges we faced in the process.

Today fundraising campaigns at colleges and universities range in scale from a few million up to $1 billion. Whether on a smaller or larger scale, the search for funds is very challenging. For our team in 1988, the question was, how do you raise $5 million? In your life and work, you may face a smaller or larger test. Let us consider some ways to succeed.

Be courageous. Fundraising is like getting food for the family; you must hunt like a lion for the resources that sustain your organization. It begins with you. Believe in your Creator, who gives you talents and abilities. Believe in the values and vision of your family, school, church, or organization. Your mind-set and passion will move you to discover people and places for relationships and resources that are needed.

Be coached. Rookies and even successful professionals in business, fine arts, sports, and many other fields depend upon coaching to bring their game to a higher level. The willingness to receive information, insight, and inspiration from those who know what you need to succeed is so important. As the saying goes, the teacher will appear when the student is ready to learn. Your teacher or coach appears in your schooling and training, in your workplace and volunteer activities, and in everyday conversations with colleagues and strangers. Hiring a coach for one-on-one assistance or institutional development in acquiring financial resources pays off too.

Be creative. Fundraising, like most fields of human endeavor, has certain basic features:

- Find friends to support you.
- Present them opportunities for investing their funds in worthwhile activities, projects, and people.
- Ask for and receive their financial assistance.
- Thank and recognize them for their support.
- Use their gifts wisely, and inform them of the results.
- Maintain your relationships with your partners. Share information with them about your success.
- Ask again for their support at appropriate times.

A fundraising and friend-raising basic is that it takes fifteen different kinds of contacts with a prospective donor to receive a gift and seven different ways to thank him or her so you keep connected. As you build on these basic principles, you can adapt them, vary them, and even disrupt them in organizing your drive for funding, your marketing to specific investors, and your teamwork efforts with colleagues and volunteers.

Be committed. In a speech, Judy described her life and artwork with the theme "Life is a journey, not just a destination." She waited twenty-five years for me to be a college president and to purchase her crystal and china. She emerged as a leader as a teacher in several schools, was president of the Metro Arts Alliance in Des Moines, and was a gracious hostess to campus and community groups. Since childhood, she had desired to be an artist; she went on to earn her Bachelor of Fine Arts degree at the age of sixty and began a new business as a weaver of beautiful garments.

Commitment is a lifetime journey to achieve your dreams. Fundraising is more than courageously asking a prospective donor for a major gift. It involves building a long-term relationship with promising friends and partners. Get better acquainted with them. Listen, learn their values, and explore their desire to provide support. Give them valuable information and service. You can do so in both customary and unusual ways.

David Burrier, who was on the development staff at Grand View College, branded himself in a memorable way. He was not the tallest man around, but he stood out because he sometimes walked around with a big button on his lapel. The statement on the button was short and significant: "I'm Number 2." It brought an immediate response from people he met. They would say, "If you're Number 2, who is Number 1?" David would grin, extend his hand for a handshake, and say, "Well, you are Number 1. May I be of service to you in some way?"

Did this approach actually work? Again and again it opened the door for building a relationship that took time and paid off later. Thanks to David's good work with Alice Humphrey, she made the major lead gift of $1 million for the renovation of Old Main at Grand View College, which happened after the completion of the Agenda for Achievement Campaign.

Between a creative opening and successful closing for a gift is a process that requires commitment. You must continue to cultivate the relationship before it pays dividends. That's the way it works with human nature and the growth process. Patience and persistence are needed. This lesson was brought home to me season after season as I grew up on our Puotinen family farm. Get the field ready. Fertilize. Plant the seed. Water and weed. Pray for a good growing season. Harvest in late summer. Give thanks. Next spring, repeat the process. Plant potatoes in the same field, but rotate the grain to be grown in adjoining fields. Understanding natural cycles can also help fundraisers in their field approach the art and science of harvesting good gifts.

Remember the 15/7 rule: fifteen contacts with a person to receive a gift and seven ways to thank them for their generous investment in your success. Persist with the process. Don't give up. Continue your commitment. You may need to ask for the gift several times.

Here's an example to illustrate the four points above. It's the story of the Dan Krumm Business Center at Grand View College.

Be courageous. Consultant Ron Mulder said we needed two lead donor prospects to chair the new $5 million Agenda for Achievement campaign. We reviewed the listing of Grand View trustees who were donors to the college and very familiar with the college's heritage and vision. Two trustees agreed to be cochairs for the campaign and one stepped forward to provide the largest campaign gift.

This positive response came from a Grand View trustee, Daniel Krumm. He was president and CEO of Maytag Corporation, a regional business leader and philanthropist, and a dedicated Lutheran layman in his home church in Newton, Iowa. He and his wife, Ann, were active in charitable giving and had decided to focus their gifts in the areas of education, church organizations, and special causes.

Be creative. The major Krumm gift came in several stages. They made an initial family gift of five figures. Dan invited our written proposals and presentations to be made to the Maytag Company and the Maytag Foundation. His advocacy ensured funding from both organizations at a major level. There was a way to go before reaching the $1 million mark. As a campaign cochair, Dan encouraged other local business leaders and their companies to provide major gifts for the campaign. It is common practice for key business leaders to seek financial support for their individual priority projects that would benefit the community and its institutions.

Dan leveraged his gift and influence among his fellow Grand View board members in another way. He fueled the Agenda for Achievement campaign bus with another commitment. He joined John Bachman, a fellow board member and TV news anchor in Des Moines, and me in creating a video presentation specially designed for all board members. John Bachman made a simulated TV news broadcast in the Grand View Cowles Communication Center with both of us; it included some surprising news. Dan announced his challenge gift of an additional $100,000 if his fellow Grand View board members would match that amount in several months. Each trustee received a videotape of the interview and a pledge card. This creative presentation encouraged trustees to go the second mile in matching Dan's challenge gift. It worked.

Recognizing Dan's leadership efforts led the Grand View board of trustees to name the future business, accounting, and computer-science academic building in his honor. The design and construction of the new building became a team effort involving an architectural firm, contractors, city officials, college administration, faculty members, students, and alumni for input in the construction process. The eventual design included a central auditorium with tiered tables and seating, smaller classrooms, computer science labs, and faculty offices in a one-story building. Accessible to students and faculty, technologically equipped, and functional for instruction and public events, the Daniel Krumm Business Center became an excellent new academic and community resource. Its construction, dedication, and opening followed the completion of a structural renovation of the existing Grand View College Library as part of the Agenda for Achievement campaign.

Be committed. The Dan Krumm legacy is evident in his commitment to his family, his church, and his community. He and Ann were life partners that shared their values with their children, such as Tim, who later became a Grand View trustee. Dan was the director of a forty-voice church choir, and during his years of business travel, he returned for every choir rehearsal and performance. His leadership was highly regarded in the greater Des Moines community.

Being a president and CEO brings its own set of stress and setbacks. When visiting Dan's home, I noticed a saying on a kitchen plaque in the Krumm kitchen that read, "When all else fails, there is always the garden." Dan was an avid gardener who grew many kinds of flowers, especially roses. They reminded him of God's goodness and the beauty in God's creation. Eventually he decided to retire after a distinguished career at Maytag and to devote himself to volunteer service in his church and community. Then he became afflicted with cancer, which eventually took his life, but his legacy as a lion lives on. He unleashed his courage, creativity, and commitment to make life better for those who follow.

Be coached. Dan mentored me and many others in the process of raising funds for Grand View College. You may have someone like Dan in your life, and there are others too. Some are volunteers that step up to assist you. In the Agenda for Achievement campaign, board presidents Robert Larson and Garland Carver introduced me to business leaders one-on-one and in group settings. I accompanied them in recruiting new board members, and we made presentations together for major donor prospects. Key alumni leaders well versed in the Danish American traditions enabled me to understand and appreciate the heritage of the "happy Danes" that founded Grand View College.

Organizational leaders are often well served by paid consultants. Ron Mulder of Gonser Gerber Advancement Consultants guided our efforts in the Agenda for Achievement campaign, focused attention on key relationships and action steps, and regularly evaluated our results. Walker Johansson of Washington, DC, spent some time with us on strategic planning and marketing. He encouraged us to go further than developing a three-year plan to envisioning what Grand View College could be in ten to twenty years.

Gary Quehl, formerly of the Council of Independent Colleges, interviewed our college and local business leaders and cautioned me to focus on the primary goals of the Agenda for Achievement campaign, rather than pursuing additional projects, such as renovation of Old Main and creation of an expanded physical education center with community fitness services. These projects were undertaken in subsequent years.

Finally, Bill Miller Associates of Salem Virginia spent several months with us designing a new approach to student recruitment and financial aid strategies. Byron Tweeten, CEO of Growth Design Corporation in Milwaukee, gave us development coaching following the Agenda for Achievement Campaign. The counsel of these various professionals provided perspectives and strategies to review and adapt into a more comprehensive approach to designing the future of Grand View College.

You Create New Ventures

Identify a new project, program, or structure that you and your team can create, find funds for, and complete for the good of your family, organization, or community.

Suggestions for Getting and Giving a Million

- **Determine the long- and short-term financial goals** for your group or organization to meet a major institutional need. Interviews with constituents help identify those needs and shape your strategy. Then write a case statement to introduce the campaign.

- **Identify the key leaders for the campaign** that are fully committed to the project. Before public announcement of the campaign, complete the solicitation of major gifts. Organize staff and volunteers to handle communications and to conduct both large and small events. Prepare publications for the campaign.

- **Spend time researching what other organizations are doing.** Brainstorm money-generating ideas; consider everything from direct mail and monthly giving programs to large silent auctions, benefit concerts, and merchandising campaigns. Cull through the resulting list for feasibility, expense, and probable return outcomes.

- **Get to know your potential donors** by inviting them to organizational programs, events, and focus group sessions on the campaign goals and projects that excite them and would appeal to the wider constituency. Establish categories of donors, such major donors, alumni, businesses, faith-based organizations, and friends.

- **Create and implement strategies,** such as specific major events, publications, meetings, and mailings to those categories. Speak to them about different giving levels that are available. Identify the major presenters for public events.

- **Launch the fundraising campaign.** Make it a festive, gala experience. Announce the total amount of major gifts already received. Highlight the event in the local media and organizational publications. Begin solicitation of funds from every donor group.

- **Build the campaign momentum from the launch.** Lead and motivate organizational representatives and volunteers to complete their individual contacts with prospective donors and other efforts to move the campaign forward. Publicize major gifts and special naming opportunities in campaign buildings and projects.
- **Get the message out clearly and professionally.** If you are creating a large newsletter, e-update, or direct mail to donors, make sure they are well written, to the point, and make good use of graphics. If no one in your organization is a writer, solicit a volunteer or hire a writer to take on the task.
- **Publicize major events and activities,** such as the completion of new building construction and renovation, the start-up of new projects and products, and honoring people for their service and financial support. Highlight publicly the reaching of campaign goals.
- **Thank all donors, volunteers, leaders, and staff** for their contributions to making the campaign successful. Remember, seven or more ways to thank and involve people and build the foundation for future fundraising campaigns as needed and deemed feasible.
- **Review and assess all phases** of the completed campaign, the performance of paid and volunteer leaders, and the ingathering of pledged gifts. Update your information databases. Consider strengths and weaknesses of your campaign efforts, and make recommendations for how to make it better in the next major campaign and in annual-fund solicitations.

CHAPTER 8

Build Your Master Plan

Lions have two main hunting methods. In a version of the game Grandmother's Footsteps, the lions move from cover to cover with a final burst of speed at the end. They find a bush close to something their prey needs—usually water—and then climb in and wait. There's an added advantage to this: the lions catch up on sleep, though technically they are "out hunting." Lions are good at hiding, and they are phenomenally patient.

Lions plan their hunts in a way that causes them to succeed and thrive. Leaders plan their work to achieve success and sustainability. Lions strategize and work to catch their prey. Leaders and teams take decisive actions for desired results. Lions are persistent and patient. Leaders use time and resources efficiently.

A version of an old proverb says, "A vision without work remains a dream, work without vision is drudgery, but vision combined with work leads to victory."

> *You Get Started*
>
> Share your first experience in planning and doing a major event or project and the results you achieved and lessons you learned.

My first experience with an organized strategic planning effort happened at Lenoir-Rhyne College in Hickory, North Carolina. President Al Anderson led this planning endeavor in the late 1970s to ensure the college's solvency, success, and sustainability. Many planning models exist for higher education. Al believed the business-planning models would benefit Lenoir-Rhyne, so he sought guidance from the college's board of trustees chairman. This CEO of a major firm in Charlotte, North Carolina, showed him a successful business design.

President Anderson presented the strategic planning model to his administrative cabinet, and we gathered five years of institutional data in admissions, revenues/expenditures, fundraising, educational programs, and personnel. We also identified various trends in institutional performance. Extended conversation ensued about the college's external environment in North Carolina and about the internal environment on campus with student activities, faculty development, and staff support. Patiently we talked at length about the mission, vision, and brand of the college, and we identified various strengths, weaknesses, opportunities, and threats evident at Lenoir-Rhyne.

Critical questions emerged as we considered the next five years. Should current educational programs and student activities, such as intercollegiate sports, be maintained, modified, or discontinued? What new directions for Lenoir-Rhyne could be developed in various areas of the college's operations and services? We identified a dozen possibilities, and Assistant to the President Jeff Norris prepared a brief proposal with cost/benefit analyses for each one. He worked with President Anderson and others to edit and refine various drafts developed over the summer. It became a strategic plan, called Education through Engagement.

We rolled out the first draft of the plan at the first faculty meeting in August, and we encountered criticism for not sufficiently involving faculty leaders in the planning process. They challenged the absence of specific information concerning which faculty and staff positions would be restructured and/or downsized. Such personnel changes, primarily for cost containment and program redirection, needed further conversation and refinement. Our administrative team then sought information and input from various stakeholders and colleagues to create a stronger, more successful plan.

The four division chairs in humanities, business, human services, and education worked with me as the academic dean. We sought information and assistance from the Lenoir-Rhyne faculty and staff in further refining the academic portions of the plan. Robust dialogue and teamwork resulted in several changes to the college curriculum, such as a new core curriculum based on Education through Engagement aims. We created several new academic majors and an evening college program for a new adult student clientele. These new educational offerings attracted students and provided high-quality programs to prepare them for graduate studies and employment in a competitive marketplace.

The evening Tuesday-N-Thursday adult education program was launched in 1980. It enrolled a new market of older students who had jobs during the day and needed an accelerated evening program to earn their college degrees. Our marketing slogan was "Put some TNT in your life and career." Leading to baccalaureate degrees in business, education, social services, and other fields, the TNT program enabled adults to take two classes on Tuesday and Thursday each week from 6:00 to 10:00 p.m. during an eight-week period.

Students needed to work hard and smart while holding day jobs, taking classes, and caring for family members. They liked the program because they could complete four courses in sixteen weeks—the average course load during a semester for day students. This schedule fit federal guidelines for being a full-time student and qualified them for student financial aid, such as the Pell Grant and scholarships. The program continued to grow.

In addition to institutional planning, we initiated a process for individual faculty and staff members to complete their own personal strategic plan with individual mission statements, visions for life and work, three- to five-year goals, self-assessment, and other dimensions. This effort prompted important reflection and lively conversations. The Lenoir-Rhyne women's basketball coach used this approach with her team members in a successful season that brought them to the Final Four NAIA championship tournament in Ohio. A male faculty member took a lighter approach to the assignment by having a personal goal of having an active sex life at the age of seventy-five. Overall, the institutional and individual strategic planning undertaken at Lenoir-Rhyne College provided foundational planning experiences for those that participated.

You Create Your Plan

Take some time to develop a written statement that includes your vision for the future, your purpose/mission, your strengths and weaknesses, your main goals, and your action plans for the next six months or longer.

Now we fast-forward from 1983 in North Carolina to 1988 in Des Moines, where strategic and campus master planning became more comprehensive, creative, and visionary. Organizational leaders need coaches or consultants to give valuable counsel on transactional details of ongoing operations and transformative suggestions to take you to a new level. Marketing consultant Walker Johansson of Washington, DC, helped us with his campus interviews of leaders. He encouraged combining strategic planning and marketing. He made recommendations for advertising, publications, and student recruitment. We initially thought about developing a five-year strategic plan, but Walker encouraged Grand View leaders to envision the college campus and its educational programs ten to twenty years down the road.

From time to time, individuals, committees, and even organizations engage in conversations about the future. Random suggestions, specific ideas, and well-formulated plans regarding one aspect of an organization can occur and even be implemented. It is possible to take good intentions, concerns for improvements, and organizational suggestions to a new level. An accelerated planning activity can result in breakthrough thinking by a dedicated group of people with purpose and commitment.

At Grand View College, we experienced a campus master-planning process reminiscent of a mastermind approach. Napoleon Hill, author of *Think and Grow Rich*, first defined the mastermind as a "coordination of knowledge and effort, in a spirit of harmony, between two or more people, for the attainment of a definite purpose."[16] Andrew Carnegie, a wealthy steel magnate, used this concept frequently in advancing his business in the manufacturing and marketing of steel. The benefits of having a supportive mastermind group are numerous:

- You have a group of people available to help you succeed.
- You get the benefit of differing perspectives, input, and feedback.

- Your mastermind team brings resources and connections to the table you might not have had on your own.
- You receive accountability and inspiration from the group, thus enabling you to maintain focus in achieving your goals.

During a three-day period in May of 1991, we experienced such a mastermind event at Grand View College. We needed a campus master plan. Construction of the new Dan Krumm Business Building had inspired a review of campus buildings and grounds. A bird's-eye view, a campus map, and a walkabout all revealed the nature of our urban campus. Grandview Avenue, in the heart of the campus, extended to the west and the east as a key corridor, with the main administrative and classroom buildings and library of Grand View College situated alongside a Lutheran church, senior care facility, and several private homes.

Eastward on Grandview Avenue, it is bisected by Fourteenth Street, a busy north-south thoroughfare with considerable car and truck traffic. This created a pedestrian safety issue at Fourteenth Street. A stoplight at the intersection became the port of entry to the east side of the campus, which included several buildings, athletic fields, and a gymnasium. Separate residence halls for men and women and programs in art and theater in the student center emphasized both academic and student-life activities. Intercollegiate and intramural baseball, basketball, soccer, and volleyball brought participants and fans to this area of the campus.

The architectural firm hired by Grand View College recommended revisiting the campus master plan for a long-term vision and coordinated a creative approach for this task: the "charette" concept of planning and design. Though this dynamic concept originated at the École des Beaux-Arts in Paris in the nineteenth century, the word *charrette* comes from the French word for "cart" or "chariot." Student architects worked urgently as teams at the end of a term to complete their projects. A charrette, or cart, was wheeled among the students to pick up their work for review while each one worked furiously to apply finishing touches on projects to place *en charrette*, in the cart.[14]

The college architect organized a three-day master-planning event at the college, and his team included himself as key moderator and two graphic artists to provide sketches of campus design elements resulting from information and insights in group brainstorming and discussion.

The planning group included representatives from various constituencies of Grand View: administration, board of trustees, development board, alumni, faculty, and students. The city representatives were the mayor, city council members, and Union Park Neighborhood Association leaders. Participants enthusiastically offered suggestions, concerns, and historical references to the design of a new campus master plan.

On the second day, everyone received written summaries of suggestions and were excited to see them in the visionary sketches by the graphic artists. A faculty member had remembered that a duck pond was part of the landscape near his residence hall at the college he had attended. Voila! The next day a duck pond appeared in the sketches for the landscaping near the residence halls. It was given careful consideration but not included in the final version.

Some elements of the emerging plan grew from prior explorations, such as the renovation of the historic Old Main of Grand View College, the expansion of the athletic facilities with provision for community fitness programs, additional academic buildings, and residence halls. The matter of the intersection of Grandview Avenue and Fourteenth Street received serious consideration. Should the college continue the current practice, or should there be an underground passage from one side of the street to the other? Should an overpass walkway be created for people to walk across?

These questions remained unresolved for others to consider later. In 2013, Grand View University President Kent Henning led a major effort to plan the construction of that overpass. Under his leadership, Grand View updated campus master planning and completed construction of the Johnson Wellness Center, the Rasmussen Center for Community Advancement Professions, and new student housing. Construction of a new student center is underway.

Many other ideas and suggestions relating to campus beautification, college and community partnerships, and academic and student-life programs grew from the three-day charrette. The charette experience and its visual product became an important stepping-stone to the future.

You Change Your Environment

Meet with an architect, environmental designer, and contractor to envision a plan to improve your campus site or home for your organization or family.

Our family of five once experienced strategic planning in a festive mode. We had a Christmas Eve dinner tradition of enjoying a leisurely beef fondue meal and conversation. The Christmas meal in 1993 included our daughters at home for the holiday. Anne had graduated from the University of Chicago undergraduate program and was enrolled in the Art Institute of Chicago as a first-year painting student. A graduate of Augustana College in Rock Island, Illinois, Marji was a master's degree student in Environmental Management at Duke University. Sara was a student at Gustavus Adolphus College in Saint Peter, Minnesota.

During the mealtime conversation, each family member reflected about the year closing and one-by-one shared their top three achievements and/or blessings from their year. It seemed to go well, so we identified our top three goals for the coming year. Our mini-charrette experience created a family mind-set of mutual affirmation, goal awareness, and personal support. We decided to continue this tradition.

At one Christmas Eve mealtime, all three daughters had significant others, and they were eager to talk about their guys. Coincidentally Fred Grandy, one of the stars of TV's popular show *Love Boat*, had left the program to run for office as governor of Iowa. It was delightful to report that Grandy might be stumping to be governor while I was the captain of the Puotinen love boat.

Like so many parents, Judy and I had wondered how we could send our three daughters to college. We believed their continuing education was a major priority in our family strategic planning. Anne, Marji, and Sara were hard-working, bright students, so they qualified for some scholarships. We provided them financial assistance, and because of my position, Marji and Sara were able to benefit from a tuition-free exchange program among Evangelical Lutheran Church in America colleges as they attended Augustana College and Gustavus Adolphus College, respectively. This reciprocal tuition benefit was available for many faculty, staff, and administrators of participating colleges. Needless to say, this was a boon for our family during a nine-year period. All three daughters graduated from their colleges and pursued graduate study at the master's and doctoral levels by their own efforts.

Getting back to the love boat: all three daughters became engaged to their beau's within a few months—Anne and Yazid Ebeid in early January, Marji and Mick Hartcher in March, and Sara and Scott Anderson in December. Judy worked creatively and effectively with

111

all three daughters to plan their weddings, which occurred in a space of eighteen months. My task was to be the officiating pastor at each event and to find financial resources to help everything happen.

In December of 1994, University of Chicago alumni Anne and Yazid were married in Bond Chapel at the University of Chicago, with the reception on campus. His parents, Ibrahim and Maria Ebeid, his sister, Carolina, and graduate friends from Tulane University were among the honored guests. They joined the Puotinen family and friends for this joyous event.

The following December of 1995, Marji and Mick had a wedding ceremony outdoors in Newcastle, just north of Sydney, Australia. They had met while working in Townsville on the beautiful Great Barrier Reef. We provided travel and lodging for Anne, Sara, and their beaus.

In June of the next year, Sara and Scott were married in St. John's Lutheran Church in Des Moines. His parents, Darwin and Carol Anderson, were honored guests. And forty Gustavus Adolphus classmates attended; a brass ensemble from their group provided special music.

These three festive family events prepared us all for the future, when we would weather several storms, including flooding and a financial crisis that began in 1993.

You Celebrate Family Plans

Take time with your family to view and/or create your family pictures, albums, and videos of memorable events from school, church, home, travel, and elsewhere.

Suggestions for Building a Master Plan

- **Define the overall objective of the project,** and summarize it in one or two sentences at the top of your project plan. Give the project a catchy yet relevant name so you can easily refer to it when discussing progress with your employees or team members.
- **Decide on the team leader for the project or facilities plan.** A clearly defined point person for coordinating the planning process, organizing the participants, gathering the information, and summarizing the results is essential. Once completed, the planning document goes to other decision makers for review, authorization to proceed, funding, and other elements.
- **Contract with certain professionals,** such as architects, graphic designers, and others with expertise relevant to your needs. The arrangements can vary from a few hours of their time to a more extensive commitment.
- **Identify the people** for the planning team and for focus groups. Include all constituent groups in the process. Invite them to participate. Indicate that their overall effort will be important and timely. If you do a charette, it can be done in three to five days.
- **Do some research.** Examine the existing and prior plans of the organization. Review master planning information from other organizations that are available online. Summarize your findings into a brief planning document and/or PowerPoint presentation.
- **Convene a meeting of all planning participants.** Explain the purpose and process involved in that particular plan. Provide them information gleaned from initial research. Do a team-building exercise to generate trust and participation.
- **Continue the momentum from the first session.** Start by having breakout groups of five or six people. Challenge them

113

to imagine the possibilities for the organization. Use the 10-10-10 method by having them imagine or brainstorm their top-ten lists. List what can be accomplished in ten years, and pick three priorities for the next ten weeks.

- **Gather the findings from each group.** Receive written notes from them. Have a representative mention three possibilities in a reporting session for everyone. Give all information to the leader of the process, the architect, the graphic artist, or other professionals for further refinement into a visual depiction of possibilities.

- **Review the refinement report.** Take time to consider various options and to identify the primary directions and goals for the emerging plan of action. The give-and-take among the group members will sharpen the vision and excite the participants.

- **Define the step-by-step tasks** that need to be completed to achieve your goals. Determine a budget for each task as well as tools or resources that will be needed to complete the task. Estimate a timeline for each task with the desired deadlines for completion.

CHAPTER 9

Recover from a Crisis

Lions live in groups known as prides, which are composed of up to three males, about a dozen females, and their lion cubs. A pride's females are generally responsible for hunting so that the pride can eat; they do so by working together.

In the pride, it is the job of the male lion to defend the pride's turf. A lion's courage is tested when a predator confronts it and the tribe. Overcoming the threat of a predator tests the resolve, the skills, and the strength of the lion. For the lion in the jungle, the threat generally comes on the ground. President Teddy Roosevelt said, "Lions are boldest when the night is the darkest."

What if the threat comes from the air, as it does sometimes for the human community? The test is to unleash the lion in you to protect your pride, family, and community.

You Defend Yourself

Remember a time when you faced threat or opposition, and note how you responded to this crisis.

New York Mayor Rudy Giuliani is an internationally recognized and admired lion. The terrorist attack on the Twin Towers on September 11, 2001, became a major crisis that tested Giuliani's leadership and courage. In his landmark book, *Leadership,* Giuliani describes how he led a team of New York City staff members, first responders, volunteers, and others to recover from this unprecedented crisis.[17]

Reading his book brings back vivid images of that fateful day and of the emotions people felt throughout our country and elsewhere. Hearing the mayor's own voice tell the story of that day underscores the high standard of courage and leadership he set for all leaders to follow.

Giuliani was the keynote speaker at the JT Foxx Mega Partnering IV conference in Chicago, where he described the challenges he faced and listed five principles. "The first principle," he said, "is having a set of beliefs and knowing what they are." He cited President Ronald Reagan and Martin Luther King Jr. as men who displayed this characteristic and used it to bring about change.

Courage is the second principle. According to Mayor Giuliani, "Courage is not the absence of fear. Courage is feeling fear and being able to overcome it," as the firefighters who went into the World Trade Center did. Optimism is essential to courage.

The third principle is relentless preparation. Giuliani said, "If you prepare for everything else relentlessly, you will be able to respond to the unexpected as if intuitively." On September 11, he realized that his emergency-response people were in uncharted territory, but as their response evolved, he realized that they had already prepared for the various disasters that were simultaneously unfolding.

Number four is teamwork. "No leader ever operates on his own or her own," he said. A leader needs to know his or her strengths and weaknesses and figure out how to counterbalance the weaknesses. "All human institutions have them," he said about weaknesses.

Finally, a leader needs to communicate. "You've got to be able to talk to people and express what you believe," the Mayor concluded. "If you're there for them, they'll be there for you. You've got to show caring for the people who work with you if you want them to go above and beyond the call of duty."

You Follow Your Leader

Share how you used any of Rudy Giuliani's five key principles to deal with a major crisis or problem that you faced.

Leaders encounter crises of various kinds, and some are larger and farther-reaching than others. The Flood of 1993 in the Midwest is an example, and here is a personal story of how it impacted the Des Moines area, Grand View College, and my leadership team.

In July, Judy and I were returning from a trip to Europe as a Rotary Exchange Couple. We had spent several weeks in various cities in Finland with Rotarians, followed by trips to Berlin and the Czech Republic, where we met with leaders of the University of Southwest Bohemia and established an exchange agreement regarding faculty and students. It was a good trip, and we were eager to return home.

We landed in Chicago's O'Hare Airport and then boarded the flight homeward. As the plane traversed the countryside and came closer to Des Moines, we saw below the flooding of major rivers.

An overview of this crisis includes these environmental parameters: A rainy autumn in 1992 resulted in above-normal soil moisture and reservoir levels in the Missouri and Upper Mississippi River basins. During the winter of 1992–93, the region experienced heavy snowfall. Persistent storms bombarded the Upper Midwest with voluminous rainfall the subsequent spring. Soils across much of the affected area were saturated by June 1, with additional rainfall all running off into streams and rivers, instead of soaking into the ground. July brought more heavy rain to the Missouri and Upper Mississippi River basins in Missouri, Iowa, Kansas, Nebraska, North and South Dakota, Illinois, and Minnesota. Rainfall amounts of five to seven inches (125 to 175 mm) in twenty-four hours were common.

Recalling in 2013 the impact of this flood on the Des Moines Water Works twenty years ago, Pat Ripley wrote in a blog,

> At 3:02 a.m. on July 11, 1993 Des Moines Water Works shut down operations after the water treatment plant and general office were inundated with flood water. It all began July 8, when 8-10 inches of rain fell in the upper Raccoon River watershed. On July 9, the levee was closed. At 1:00 a.m. on July 11, water started coming over the levee. The Raccoon River crested at the historic level of 26.75 feet, 1.75 feet higher than the levee.

> The dewatering process began along with restoration of the high voltage and high service pumps, chemical feeds, and refilling the distribution system. The National Guard air-lifted equipment in and out of the treatment plant. Staff worked round-the-clock. The general office was relocated. Seven days later DMWW began pumping potable water from the Fleur Drive plant. Customers could use the water for sanitary use on Day 12, and the water was safe to drink on Day 19.[18]

After describing the recovery operation, she detailed some restructuring initiatives that took place:

> The levee around the water treatment plant was heightened by 6 feet. Permanent flood gates have been installed. A second treatment plant, the L.D. McMullen Water Treatment Plant at Maffitt Reservoir, began operation in 2000. A third treatment plant, the Saylorville Water Treatment Plant went online in 2011.

Recovery. Restructuring. Then thoughts about renewal. She concluded,

> DMWWW was forever changed by the Flood of 1993. The product we produce daily became even more important, and our commitment to quality and service became even stronger. The dedicated employees, tireless volunteers, and the utility's commitment to the community allowed us to quickly recover, restore service and rebuild to bring the community safe, reliable, high quality water now and in the future.

During the recovery period, July 11–22, the Army National Guard and American Red Cross set up water stations, and the local Anheuser-Busch distributor contributed water in white six-packs with its logo on it. Once running water was restored, there was enough pressure for people to bathe and flush toilets, but the water was not certified potable until July 29. The final usage restrictions were lifted in August.

Major sandbagging activities took place at various venues. Local and national leaders led citizens of all ages, volunteers, and college students in this effort. My sandbagging experiences provided some memorable lessons about leadership. Sandbags came in various sizes and weights. The leader of our lineup of sandbaggers gave us a heads up on the weight of each sandbag as they came down the line one by one. "This one is a poodle ... Now here comes a German shepherd ... Look out; this one's a Saint Bernard." One afternoon, President Bill Clinton arrived on the scene, along with a group of national TV news anchors and reporters, to view the efforts and shake hands with numerous volunteers.

Jim Aipperspach, the president of the United Way of Central Iowa, convened a community task force to work on the fall 1993 United Way drive. It's always a challenge to set the goal for a funding campaign, and we liked the suggestion of a fellow task-force member: "Let's make the goal $11,111,111, because every one counts." Many generous hearts, helpful hands, and urgent voices worked together to go above that goal. Appearing before several community groups to ask for financial support, we emphasized the overall goal of everyone being involved. As I related my sandbagging experience in several community settings, my request to support the United Way drive financially concluded, "Your gift can be the size of a Saint Bernard or a German shepherd or a poodle, because every one counts."

The disastrous Flood of 1993 curtailed or slowed many city functions in Des Moines. Economic hardships in central Iowa forced nontraditional students to refocus their priorities and rebuild their homes, businesses, and communities. Several colleges experienced student enrollment downturns. Although floodwaters in Des Moines did not inundate the campus of Grand View College, its impact was felt, for ninety fewer full-time students than the projected amount enrolled for classes. On September 21, 1993, a total of 1,377 students registered at Grand View College with 987 as full-time day students and the remainder as part-time enrollees. As primarily a commuter campus with many working adult students, the local disruptions to the environment and economy impacted our college operations. A preliminary budgetary assessment projected a shortfall of upwards of $1 million in revenues for the budget year that extended from September 1993 to August 1994.[19]

This sobering news prompted our administrative team to begin an appropriate response to our situation. My team included the vice presidents for academic affairs, business, and development along with the director of admissions, dean of students, campus pastor, and assistant to the president. We transmitted information as soon as possible on the institutional crisis to the faculty, staff, and trustees. I announced, "In education we are accustomed to the three Rs— reading, 'riting, and 'rithmentic. Now we need to learn the new three Rs of recovery, restructuring, and renewal."

After intense conversations among ourselves and with faculty and staff colleagues, we proposed the Grand View Recovery Plan, which was approved by the board of trustees on October 15, 1993. The plan included three key goals with several strategies that projected monetary results:

- increase college revenue by $300,000 over the revised 1993–1994 budget projection
- reduce college expenditures by $300,000 under the revised budget
- provide administrative oversight for attaining a balanced 1993–94 budget and for developing a long-range strategic plan

The college-wide recovery effort eventually led to achieving a year-end 1993–94 actual budget with an $85,000 shortfall rather than a million-dollar one.

You Recover from Setbacks

Share your key strategies for cutting your costs and increasing your revenue to solve a financial crisis in your workplace, community group, or family.

During the recovery year, Grand View College developed a new strategic plan. A Business & Accounting Department faculty member joined our administrative team, which expanded its outreach and communication with members of the college community. This group, with five additional academic and staff divisional areas, now comprised a steering committee. Together we developed a new vision, mission statement, and affirmation of core values to guide the planning effort. Three future options emerged for consideration:

- An *amplification* model, called Grow & Grow, projected building the college enrollment to 1,500.
- A *restructure* plan, identified as the Trim & Grow model, envisioned a stable enrollment of 1,377 students for the coming year.
- A *retrenchment* alternative, known as Trim & Cut, anticipated 1,150 students in the near term.

The retrenchment alternative was a backup option if needed in the future. The amplification model seemed possible in future years. The restructure option appeared to be necessary for the next one to three years.

The restructuring plan for college operations began taking shape in November 1993. Administrative team members met with their department heads to identify potential reductions in personnel positions, salary adjustments, and other nonpersonnel cost-containment strategies in all departments of the college. Admissions and financial aid staff intensified their student recruitment efforts. Development staff worked with me to alert alumni and friends of the enrollment shortfall and the need for increased annual-fund support. Trustees stepped forward with their guidance and financial support during this post flood crisis.

The preparation of the 1994–95 fiscal budgets tested the resolve, patience, and goodwill of Grand View employees as more detailed information on the restructuring plan was shared with them. Several face-to-face meetings with faculty and staff were held, and they received written and oral statements for their review and response. In larger group meetings, I accepted responsibility for the college's circumstances and tough decisions. At times it felt like being a lightning rod with the strong emotions of colleagues going up and down my spine.

The most controversial proposal in the restructuring plan called for each employee to take a 2 percent salary reduction for 1994–95. The reduction made a balanced budget for the next year feasible, but it was demoralizing for many staff. In hindsight, a plan to keep all salaries level for 1995–96 would have fared better.

Some important lessons about salary adjustments occurred during my presidential tenure. In my first weeks on campus in 1988, the Des Moines mayor shared the advice given to him by his predecessor: Promise very little as you begin your work, because constituents will be glad when there is progress, and they will be more understanding of what you must do in difficult times. It all comes back to you.

Some campus colleagues strongly encouraged me in 1988 to build salary increases into planning based on increasing student enrollment. We included salary adjustments in the Agenda for Achievement campaign. The level of increases became a key issue in subsequent years. This rookie college president pushed the envelope. At a faculty meeting in 1988, I announced a goal of seeking to raise faculty and staff salaries by 24 percent over a three-year period at a rate of 8 percent per year. As it happened, salaries increased by 7.8 percent in the first year, 6.2 percent in the second year, and 5.2 percent in the third year. These gains were offset by the 2 percent decrease adopted for the 1994–95 academic year.

Being a leader requires a strong mind and a good heart. The planning outcomes for 1994–95 called for restructuring or reducing some personnel positions. The thirteen personnel moves were equally divided between the faculty and staff. Administrative vice presidents and deans met initially with their team members facing these moves. I also met with them to thank them for their service and to offer them assistance from the college. Three senior faculty members willingly accepted early retirement offers. Some part-time faculty positions were reduced or eliminated. Several staff reductions were made.

These personnel changes understandably had an impact on these colleagues and their families. A person can feel hurt, rejected, and fearful when let go, especially for decisions not based on faulty performance. It is important to reach out to colleagues in these situations to affirm their value as friends in a common enterprise and to encourage them in their future endeavors.

You Receive Feedback

Share a time when you benefited from an assessment of your work and how you used it to improve your performance.

Coinciding with the 3-R Flood Recovery efforts at Grand View College, preparations for the renewal of our accreditation took place. Colleges and universities periodically undergo a systematic internal review to prepare an Institutional Self-Study with extensive assessment information, financial data, and other items. Midwestern educational institutions forward this document to the North Central Association of College and Schools (NCA). This oversight organization then selects a team of four to eight educators to visit the college campus for on-site examination of programs and facilities, interviews with key personnel and students, and discussion of their findings over several days. The NCA team generally consists of representatives from other comparable colleges or universities. In their final interview, they provide an oral report to local campus representatives and then develop a written report for transmission to the NCA. Then they make a final decision regarding an initial accreditation or renewal for the institution being reviewed.

The self-study process at Grand View College began in June of 1993, and Dr. Ferol Menzel coordinated the team effort of information gathering, group discussion, and report preparation. She served as chair of the Social and Behavioral Science Division at Grand View and also became assistant to the president during the self-study process and the 1993 Flood Recovery and Restructuring Plan. In December 1994, the Grand View College Institutional Self-Study was published and forwarded to the North Central Association of Colleges and Schools. Their team of visitors came to Grand View in March 1995, in time for formal action on reaccreditation in June of 1995.

Thanks to a college-wide team effort, Grand View College received the ten-year renewal of accreditation by North Central Association of College and School and achieved an FY 1994–95 budgetary surplus of $285,000. With joy and appreciation of this good news, at several college employee meetings my remarks concluded, "Grand View has made progress on the three Rs of recovery, restructuring, and renewal. We are moving to the three Ms. Thanks to you, we have mobilization. We have momentum. Now we move ahead to seek mo—more money."

In anticipation of the celebration of Grand View College's centennial in 1996, several important moves occurred. Retired Grand View faculty member and historian Thorvald Hanson published his updated history of the college, *That All Good Seed Strike Root: A Centennial History of Grand View College.*[20] It chronicled the Danish American heritage of the college as it moved over the years into the mainstream of private higher education in Iowa up to my presidential years. He recorded the important contributions made by American Danes in the growth and development of the college, and the strong support of the Des Moines area business community and loyal alumni. This strong foundation had served Grand View College so well that it prompted several initiatives in fundraising to bring our school to its second century of service.

You Stay Strong

Share how you added value to an organization in your remaining time on the job.

In June 1995, my presidency at Grand View College was losing momentum. Various faculty, staff, and trustees were concerned about the enrollment drop during the Flood of 1993, reductions in faculty and staff positions and salaries, and the delay in hiring two key vice presidential replacements in the areas of development and finance. During my annual performance review with the board of trustees chairman, we mutually agreed that I would step down as president following the 1995–96 academic year.

Fundraising became my major priority during my eighth and final year as president of Grand View. Academic Vice President Ronald Taylor provided valuable and effective administrative continuity for the faculty and staff during the presidential transition in that and subsequent years. Two important resources came to guide our efforts. Dr. Gary Quehl, formerly head of the Council of Independent Colleges (CIC), conducted a retreat for Grand View trustees and top administrators to create a stronger framework for trustees' evaluation of and involvement with the college fundraising efforts.

Second, Byron Tweeten and Jim Raffel of Growth Design in Milwaukee consulted with Grand View in building a stronger framework for involving trustees with our strategic planning and resource development. Byron Tweeten, my colleague from our administrative experience at Suomi College in the mid-1970s, used his extensive experience in the private and business sectors to guide us into phase 1 of a projected centennial campaign: Second Century of Service. The outgoing and incoming chairmen of the Grand View board, Ted Hutcheson and Charles Johnson were top level business and community leaders in Des Moines. They enlisted several other business leaders to join a steering committee for this first phase. From January through June 1966, this trustee team worked with Grand View administrators and our consultants to prepare case materials, host small-group presentations, and seek leadership gifts. These efforts resulted in several major gifts and new members joining the board of trustees.

The successful Agenda for Achievement Campaign and conversations with Danish American alumni leaders awakened interest and initial planning for the renovation of historic Old Main at Grand View College. Family and friends of the late Grand View President J. V. Rodholm were in the forefront of this effort with a major gift for a large community room in the upgraded facility. The major leadership gift of $1 million came from alumnus Alice Olson Humphrey. The facility underwent a complete renovation in 1998 and was named the Humphrey Center in her honor.

In retrospect, the Flood of 1993 was a watershed of challenges for the Des Moines area and Grand View College. The recovery from economic downturn, the restructuring of college operations and planning, and the renewed commitment to serve students positioned the school for its future growth. We had a leadership challenge based on the three M's: to mobilize a team effort, to build momentum to get things done, and to obtain more money.

Over eight years, our team effort raised and received $8.2 million in gift income in an extended capital and annual-fund campaign. Moreover, the endowment fund grew from $2.6 million to $4.3 million, and planned-gift expectancies increased from $1.4 million to $4 million. We doubled alumni giving. And $2 million in additional pledged gifts resulted from a team effort of president, development staff, and trustees for a first phase of the Centennial Campaign.

Judy and I began our lifelong relationship in 1964 with a dream of becoming a college presidential couple someday. Our Grand View College years from 1988–96 fulfilled that dream. My leadership was especially tested in meeting major challenges of 1993—the flood, an enrollment downturn, and fundraising. Her leadership emerged as a gracious and good host at the college and in our home, as president of Metro Arts Alliance of Des Moines, and as a caring mother of our three daughters as they transitioned into marriage and continued their education. Our courage, commitment, and caring were gifts from God for our leadership tasks. We enjoyed our journey there and began getting ready for a new dream in a new place and new challenges.

Suggestions for Surviving a Financial Crisis

- **Assess the financial damage and unknown.** Leaders need to know the key numbers of their business and the impact on the bottom line. What is the current and projected shortfall? How does loss of revenue affect the products and services you provide? What does this news do to your business and its future? How will this situation impact employee morale, investor confidence, and leadership options?

- **Gather a trustworthy team.** Transparency in examining financial records, reviewing reasons for a shortfall, and developing strategic solutions requires a team approach and ownership of the problems.

- **Seek advice and counsel from experienced professionals.** Other individuals and organizations have weathered similar financial crises. Turn-around resource people can provide valuable ideas, strategies, and support to leaders facing difficult decisions.

- **Keep your reorganization options open.** Sometimes cash-flow issues unveil deeper problems in your business, and a reorganization becomes necessary. Perhaps no one is accountable for business performance due to external forces such a flood. Maybe your structure drives up payroll costs even when revenue generation is at a standstill. Explore your best-case, worst-case, and probable-case scenarios.

- **Establish a communications plan.** The information flow within the organization and to the general public may require two types of plans. Internally the management team and departmental heads work together to contact their employees and involve them in exploring solutions. In smaller organizations, a meeting of all employees, chaired by the CEO, is useful for information sharing, building trust, and moving forward. Assign a spokesperson to speak with media that seek information on sensitive issues. Identify an administrative representative to inform constituents, customers, and others that desire information about your financial challenges and plans.

- **Develop a four- to five-month cash-flow plan.** The ability to forecast, monitor, and perform in the short term can establish the foundation for a positive outcome during any financial crisis. This plan for a college coincides with the semester or term calendar that has a cycle of incoming tuition financial-aid revenues. It may be necessary to use your business credit line with your bank or to borrow internally from your cash reserves. Pay back your loan from the bank or from yourself as soon as possible.

- **Set up a cost reduction plan.** Create a line-item-specific, phased cost-reduction plan that can be implemented in the next six months. When doing so, note which vendors will need to be prioritized. Will you freeze disbursements? Will you reduce salaries or institute furloughs? How quickly can you revise payment terms with creditors? Identify your priority options and work on them. Extend the plan for a longer term if needed.

- **Create a revenue enhancement plan.** Review sales and marketing plans, and make changes to add more clients. Contact current customers for their feedback on desired products and services. Encourage employees and donors to provide additional donations in the near term. Secure foundation and federal grant support where applicable.

- **Face your financial crisis with courage.** Identify various fears that people have at this time. Remember the rallying words of President Franklin Delano Roosevelt, "The only thing we have to fear is fear itself." Hope for the future and faith in God and God's people offer the spiritual foundation for your move forward.

CHAPTER 10

Revive Your Life and Work

Every day in the jungle or on the plain, it's show time for the mighty lion. Hunting for food, taking care of cubs, and defending the pride must happen every day. There is no food storage; cubs need continual attention, and predators may arrive at any time. Younger lions learn these facts of life soon, mature mating lions adapt to this daily regimen, and older lions must keep in the hunt to survive, lest they have an untimely death. Wounded from battles and wiser in tactics, lions thrive as long as they are aroused to begin a new day with savvy, strength, and courage.

Many organizations need leaders with abundant spirit and an ambitious vision to stimulate active participation by members to survive and thrive in an environment with challenges, competition, and crises. Individuals and institutions can be revitalized in pursuit of a vision. Even one-hundred-year-old organizations can get a new lease on life and significance. The prophet Joel writes, "It will happen afterward, that I will pour out my Spirit on all flesh; and your sons and your daughters will prophesy. Your old men will dream dreams. Your young men will see visions" (Joel 2:28).

This chapter describes my appointment as vice president and provost to assist in transforming the two-year Suomi College in Hancock,

Michigan (founded in 1896) into the four-year Finlandia University. Creative vision, collaborative effort, and the use of sustainable resources in its environment mark the changes made by that team effort.

Recall. Finnish Americans founded Suomi College and Suomi Theological Seminary in 1896 to prepare future pastors and lay leaders for the Finnish Evangelical Lutheran Church in America, known as the Suomi Synod. In earlier years, the two-year college offered programs in liberal arts and career fields, such as accounting and business, to prepare students for employment and advancement in the American economy. The Suomi Seminary prepared and sent its graduates to serve Finnish American congregations in the United States and Canada.

Later in 1958, the Suomi Seminary relocated to the Maywood, Illinois, campus of the Lutheran School of Theology at Chicago along with two other seminaries founded by the United Lutheran Church in America and American Evangelical Lutheran Church.

Suomi College had a proud tradition and now faced student enrollment and financial challenges. During my freshman year at Suomi in 1959–60, 140 students were enrolled. Seeking new administrative leadership, the college called a new president, Rev. Ralph Jalkanen, in 1960. During his tenure of thirty years, he maintained its strong ties with the Lutheran and Finnish traditions, increased the size and diversity of the student body, and developed more career-related programs to serve an increasingly diverse campus community of around four hundred students. His skills in public speaking, fundraising, and administrative oversight increased his reputation locally and internationally, especially within Lutheran higher education and church constituencies.[21]

President Jalkanen mentored me as a student in 1960–61 and in my first administrative experience as the dean of faculty of Suomi College during 1974–78. After a remarkable lengthy tenure for a college president, Jalkanen retired in 1990. Prior to his retirement, he appointed Dr. Robert Ubbelhode to serve as the academic dean. After Jalkanen retired, a national search for a new leader ensued, and Ubbelhode was elected to be president.

You Work with Visionaries

Describe any changes you hope will happen to strengthen your workplace, community organization, and/or your family.

In setting a new course for Suomi College, Ubbelhode faced many challenges, and he invited me to join its board of trustees in 1993, during my presidency of Grand View College. Dealing with the financial challenges of the Flood of 1993 and other presidential experiences gave me some insights to share with Suomi College during its institutional reinvention. In January of 1996, Ubbelhode invited me to become the provost and chief operating officer at Suomi College, a newly created position to administer on-campus programs while he concentrated on fundraising, community activities, and new partnerships with educational institutions in Finland.

Reasons. Judy and I agreed to move to Upper Michigan to Suomi College in August of 1996 for several reasons. I desired to help my alma mater during a time of major transition. We wanted to restore our farm property, located ninety miles from the campus, during occasional weekend visits. And Judy want to enroll in Suomi College's Bachelor of Fine Arts program.

Reinvention. Ubbelhode established a strong relationship with the art and business program at the Kuopio Academy of Design in

Finland and sent a small team of Suomi College art and business faculty members to visit their counterparts there. These contacts led to the development of the first baccalaureate degree programs in art and design and business at Suomi College, the exchange of students and faculty with Kuopio Academy, and contacts with other educational institutions in Finland.

Renovation. In 1995 Sulo and Aileen Maki donated $1 million to Suomi College to enlarge and renovate its library. The major gift enabled the renovation to support four-year as well as two-year degree programs. The ground breaking took place during my first weeks on campus. Working with the architect and construction firms provided our administrative leaders hands-on experience with both the library and the renovation of adjoining academic facilities to house new art and design studios and classrooms. Completed in the late summer of 1997, the new library was twice as large as the old and was renamed the Sulo and Aileen Maki Library in honor of its benefactors.

Re-creation. Ubbelhode's vision and negotiation skills led to a joint venture and partnership involving Suomi College, the city of Hancock, and St. Joseph Hospital. The health-care institution desired a newer facility. Suomi College offered some land it owned on Quincy Hill as the new site for the hospital, and St. Joseph offered the existing hospital campus at a nominal fee to the college. Suomi envisioned future academic facilities in art and design as well as business in the vacated hospital. College architects, administrators, and faculty from the new degree programs toured the hospital and discussed various ways to upgrade and use it. The next step was to seek funds for its renovation from federal grants and loans, contracts with other participants in the structure, and private gifts. The completed project is described later in this chapter.

<hr>

Your Joint Venture Succeeds

Share how your team worked with others for mutual benefit and the common good.

<hr>

Response. To complement Ubbelhode's entrepreneurial visionary leadership, my primary goal as provost was to build participation and partnership of the campus community in the major institutional changes underway. In the fall of 1996, I initiated the 3-H mastermind experience. It began by randomly dividing all the faculty and staff into several small-group discussions on the future of the college. Employees names listed alphabetically were then numbered one to twelve sequentially so that a dozen small groups of around twelve employees became cohort discussion groups. This method sought a cross-section of opinions from faculty and staff members rather than from within departments.

Invitations were sent to everyone to attend a one-hour continental breakfast experience in October 1996. In separate sessions, each group provided information and insight on three issues: What are your *hopes* for the future of Suomi College? What are the *hurdles* that we are currently facing? And what are *helps* we can offer one another and the college to achieve its mission? The discussion cycle for each question invited each participant to offer views.

My notes from each discussion session were categorized into the key points for a summary report. All faculty and staff received the report with a request to rank all items with a 1, high priority; 2, medium priority; or 3, future consideration. This interactive process provided a foundation with some focused priorities for developing a new strategic plan to complement the reinvention vision. Further refinement led to time lines for implementation, leadership responsibilities, and needed resources for priority projects and activities. This 3-H approach appeared to work well at Suomi College, so it was used later in my parish ministry and shared with pastoral colleagues in other congregations.

You Develop a New Vision

Describe how you and team members created a new vision or plan for your organization.

Restart. The administrative officers and academic leaders were excited by the vision of new educational programs, expanded facilities, and exchange agreements with postsecondary schools in Finland. We worked well together to develop our two-year liberal arts and career programs into additional baccalaureate degree offerings from 1996–2002 in such fields as education, human services, liberal studies, and nursing to complement the lead four-year programs in art and design and business. Students seeking an associate of arts degree completed course work in the above fields and such career programs as accounting, criminal justice, and physical therapy.

The outreach efforts of the emerging Suomi College included workforce training programs for area businesses, agreements with community colleges for their students transferring into baccalaureate degree completion, and student/faculty exchange agreements with seven educational institutions in Finland. Funding for the developing educational programs with facilities and resources to support them became a high priority for the president, development staff, and trustees.

As the only private postsecondary educational institution in Upper Michigan, Suomi College welcomed a diverse student population of high school graduates and adult learners, residential and commuter students, and national and international learners. African American,

Native American, and other minorities added cultural diversity to campus life. Many students need financial aid to meet college costs, and like other private colleges, Suomi provided a variety of options: federal and state grants, federal and other loans, various scholarship programs, and college aid.

Renew. As a college of the Evangelical Lutheran Church in America, Suomi affirmed its heritage further by the funding and construction of a new chapel in the center of campus. A full-time pastor/religion professor held weekly worship services, directed religious programs, and counseled students.

To attract more students and enrich the cocurricular activities, an expanded intercollegiate athletics program included men's and women's basketball, hockey, volleyball, and subsequent additions of baseball/softball, volleyball, and track. This initiative developed fully during the presidency of Philip Johnson, who established an agreement with Hancock public schools to use their Condon athletic field for scheduled games.

You Create New Services

Share how you and your team designed and offered new programs and services to your clientele.

Replicate. The partnership of local organizations and the potential of joint ventures became a reality in the reinvention of the former St. Joseph Hospital, now a property of Suomi College, as described earlier. In developing the art and design and business baccalaureate programs, Ubbelhode and faculty members sought to utilize several elements of the Finnish model of education and business as practiced in the Kuopio polytechnic school. Academic studies combined with practical work experiences would enable graduates to be employable or to start a small business in their chosen fields. "No more starving artists" became the desired outcome.

Refine. In these formative years for new degree programs, Judy went back to school and earned her BFA in Fiber Arts in 2000. Her garment weaving and other fiber artistry progressed, and she graduated as an honor student as one of four first graduates in this new four-year program at Suomi College (now named Finlandia University). Her senior project was entitled "Life is a journey and not a destination" and featured four kimonos in a log-cabin weave. They depicted four roles in Judy's life: spouse/mother/grandmother, teacher, presidential spouse, and artist. Her exhibit and other garments she made were featured in several galleries in Michigan, Minnesota, and Wisconsin. She used her handiwork in speaking presentations she made in Michigan and Illinois concerning creativity and the soul of an artist. In Elgin, Illinois, she initiated the early stages of establishing her own business. (More about this later.)

Restoration. The former St. Joseph Hospital—a beautiful, multilevel building overlooking the Portage Canal between Hancock and Houghton—stands today as a remarkable example of visioning, partnership, and smart work. During 1996–2002, the Suomi College presidential team engaged in a preliminary architectural redesign of the facility, conversing with art and design as well as business faculty regarding their program needs in the building, seeking federal grant and private funding for the renovation, and exploring small-business incubators in the reinvented structure. It is exciting today to see how this transformation vision has moved ahead.

The former hospital, now the Jutila Center for Global Design and Business, on the banks of Portage Lake, less than a mile from the main campus, was opened in 2005. The renovated building now houses Finlandia's International School of Art & Design (ISAD) and the Lily I. Jutila Center for Global Design and Business. ISAD students enjoy spacious, modern studios and classrooms. The Jutila Center is a small-business incubator with more than thirty leasable spaces and other resources for business, including design and business consulting, rapid prototyping, and training seminars.[22]

You Expand Your Space

Share how you renovated your home, changed your workspace, or acquired a new facility to provide additional benefits and resources for your team members.

Rename. Prospective students found "Suomi" a bit confusing; it did not communicate a clear identity. Changing to "Finlandia" maintained the historic tradition and identity of the school. The option of choosing "college" or "university" created more conversation on campus. Advocates of "university" noted that international students and others found "university" more appealing and truer to a higher level of education. Those who favored "college" pointed out that four-year colleges in the United States generally adopted a "university" name after offering graduate-level education. The "university" proponents won the day, and Finlandia University (FU) now exists.

Review. Accreditation of Suomi College's two-year programs initially occurred in 1969. When the first baccalaureate degree programs were offered in 1996, the college received provisional accreditation by North Central Association of Colleges and Schools. To prepare for the next NCA visit, evaluation, and reaccreditation, it was necessary to begin an institutional self-study leading to a written report to the accrediting body. Given my prior experience with self-studies at Grand View College and Lenoir-Rhyne College, I volunteered to chair the self-study committee for NCA accreditation renewal and to edit/write the self-study report. The accrediting body's renewed emphasis on assessing and documenting the learning outcomes of students involved academic departments. We submitted the lengthy report and awaited the selection of a NCA team of visitors.

The NCA group arrived on campus for a three-day visit, conducted interviews with many constituent groups (trustees, administrators, faculty, staff, students, and alumni), and prepared a preliminary report. It contained various commendations, suggestions, and recommendations that they gave to the Finlandia administrative group orally and later in written form. North Central Association affirmed the overall quality of our fledgling university when it reaccredited Finlandia a few months later. We enjoyed a college-wide celebration upon receiving this news.

You Move On

Share how you felt and what you did when the time came to leave your team and move on.

Release. Ubbelhode intended to continue his presidency at Finlandia University, so it seemed reasonable for me to search for a presidential position elsewhere. In 2001–02 I had advanced to being a finalist in on-campus presidential interviews at a private four-year college and a public two-year college. Several semifinalist presidential interviews at other colleges were completed at off-campus sites. The old adage "If at first you don't succeed, try, and try again" is fitting here. But then, sometimes a new direction comes.

My contract with Finlandia University ended in May 2002 after my vice president and provost position was discontinued during a restructuring of administrative positions in which academic department heads became deans that reported directly to the president.

Finlandia Suggestions for Reinvention

- **Adopt a growth mind-set.** Opportunities to grow exist even for smaller and older organizations when their visionary leaders adapt existing strengths to survive and thrive.
- **Collaborate with potential partners.** Find people and organizations locally, regionally, and internationally to work with in expanding your client base, programs, and services.
- **Communicate expectations and goals.** Ambitious leaders involve employees, volunteers, and stakeholders in setting goals and action plans to carry out expectations and goals.
- **Create new programs and services.** Receive suggestions from current and future customers. Redesign existing offerings to offer added features and benefits and thereby expand the market. Launch new products with workable designs, adequate resources, and realistic timetables.
- **Develop financial resources.** Count on fees from clients for products and services. Seek contributions from donors and grants/loans from private and public funders. Partner with local organizations to create facilities and resources for more-sustainable development.
- **Focus on quality.** Design products, programs, and services to meet client needs and expectations as well as industry standards. Measure performance outcomes. Rely on external evaluators to assess organizational quality.
- **Lead with teamwork.** Delegate program or product development and implementation to teams with expertise and know-how. Provide coaching, training, and assistance throughout their process of working together.
- **Market your brand.** Suomi College changed its name to Finlandia University to attract greater awareness and give it an appeal identity, which included expanded programs and improved services.

- **Pivot when necessary.** Finlandia developed a flexible business model to adapt its programs, services, and facilities in response to market conditions.
- **Review results regularly.** Monitor departmental and institutional income and expenditures monthly. Maintain performance standards by doing performance reviews and creating improvement plans.

CHAPTER 11

Listen for the Call

Lions leave their pride for various reasons. In order to find receptive females in a new pride, sometimes adult males abandon a pride after they have stayed for about two years. Lions in groups do better at all stages of life. Even in groups, though, males have a hard life. They seldom live longer than twelve years in the wild, while females sometimes reach sixteen or older. Even when an older female loses most of her teeth, the pride will wait for her and share with her, as long as she can keep up.

When males are older, younger and stronger males oust them from the pride. Exiled males can steal from most other predators, but if they have to hunt on their own, they fare poorly and often get terrible wounds from kicks and horns. When they lose their teeth or health, or when they lose a teammate, they soon die.

The personal experience of eviction from one's family, home, life work, or familiar surroundings is both painful and promising. After thirty years of ministry in Lutheran higher education, including our long-standing ties with Finlandia University and the Copper Country, Judy and I were forced by administrative decision in May 2002 to leave the academic arena and campus ministry to explore a different pathway in life and work.

You Start Fresh

Share a time when you or a family member needed to change your attitude and actions to find a new job or relationship to renew your life and health.

After selling our beautiful Houghton home to the Michigan Tech basketball coach and his family, Judy and I decided to move ninety miles to the Puotinen family farm in Crystal Falls Township near Amasa, as I sought a new call for ministry. We personally packed most of our belongings and transported them by U-Haul trucks to the Puotinen family farm. Major furniture items were stored with a moving company in Calumet, twelve miles from Houghton. Since our farm was already fully furnished, it meant that many packing boxes of art supplies and books had to be stored in our farm barn. It had not housed any cattle since 1965, and a weatherproof roof and siding allowed it to be a storage facility

Judy and I had considered retiring there and establishing artist studios for her, as well as it becoming a summer place for our daughters and their families. These conversations intensified after the passing of my parents and our return to Upper Michigan.

Our daughter Sara and her husband, Scott, subsequently produced two video movies of our ongoing renovation work and family conversations in 2001 and 2002. Sara, Scott, and Anne assisted Judy and me in painting and upgrading the farmhouse. A local contractor, Roland Cornelia, helped me take down several nonfunctional outbuildings, repair and repaint the main barn, and complete numerous handyman tasks.

> ## *You Renovate This Old House*
>
> Share the experience of how you or a friend fixed your home or another house for restoration, resale, or recreation.

The first movie depicts our family efforts to upgrade the Puotinen farmhouse and landscaping, with interviews regarding the farm history. Judy and I contributed stories of family members, events, and projects. The second movie documented historic photos, diary materials, present-day footage, and reflective conversations about the experience of four generations of Puotinen women on the family farm. My Grandmother Johanna's photos, my mother Ines's diary and photos, Judy's perceptive and heartfelt reflections, and commentary by Sara and Anne made their experiences memorable for our family and other viewers. Sara and Scott presented their videos at several major conferences to favorable reviews by participants. These videos are available for viewing on www.room34.com.

> ## *You Receive a Call*
>
> Share the story of a time you responded to a new opportunity that changed your life.

A pastoral vacancy at First Lutheran Church in Iron River, Michigan—twelve miles from the farm—prompted my inquiry into becoming a parish pastor once again. Bishop Tom Skrenes of the ELCA Wisconsin–Upper Michigan Synod presented my name for consideration by the First Lutheran Church Council. During the subsequent interview, the council members asked that Judy and I move into the First Lutheran parsonage across the church parking lot to be part of the local community.

I accepted the congregation's call to serve as their pastor in late October 2002. At my installation worship service, Bishop Skrenes preached and said that my mission now was to love and care for the people of God at First Lutheran and in the community. I sought counsel and advice from other pastor friends about perspectives and practices that would help me fulfill my new mission.

Although the pastorate position at First Lutheran had been vacant for nearly a year, renovation of the parsonage was moving slowly, so it was not ready for immediate occupancy. I commuted twelve miles through wooded areas to and from the church to begin my work in late November. We weren't able to move into the parsonage until March 2003, when all renovation work was completed. I cleaned, painted, and prepared the parsonage basement to be Judy's art studio.

Romantic notions of living on the farm gave way to such realities as winter cold and snow, dodging deer and trees on icy roads, a frozen septic system, and lonely days for Judy while I was away in Iron River, and the burden of the farm mortgage. Yet there was celebration and joy. Immediate family members Anne and Yaz and their daughters from Chicago, Marji and her partner Glenn McCracken all the way from Australia, and Sara and Scott from Minneapolis all joined us for Christmas at the farm and at First Lutheran in 2003.

Our life in Iron River enabled me to experience the parish pastor's role in a rural town. Our Sunday morning services were broadcast on radio, we experienced some growth in membership, church property improvements were made, and community contacts bore fruit. Connecting with people at important life events and transitions enabled me to care for children in their baptism and Christian education, young couples preparing for marriage, adults facing health challenges, homebound members desiring Holy Communion, and families gathering to grieve the death of a loved one. It was a joy leading worship, offering sermons, and playing the guitar in a newly formed musical ensemble that led our second worship service. My ministry enabled me to give something back to Iron County, where I had grown up and gone to school.

You Start a New Job

Describe how you felt and what you did during your first few weeks in a new position.

Judy worked on art projects in her parsonage studio, participated in a book group, served on the local library board, and attended Sunday services and other church functions. She discovered the Apple Blossom Trail, which extended for two miles from near the parsonage to the Iron County Museum. This nature trail became our daily walking journey most days except in winter—a good tonic for body, mind, and spirit. From the spring through fall seasons, we also spent time on the family farm, welcoming family members there and taking care of the property and fields.

In the spring of 2004, Judy and I faced an impending economic reality. We could not continue maintaining the farm and paying down its mortgage on a pastor's salary. A favorite Puotinen family story recalled the day when Elias and Johanna Puotinen and their children burned the original mortgage on the Puotinen farm. We regretted telling our three daughters at our family reunion in June that we needed to sell it. They supported us in this decision and dealt with it as best they could. Anne and Sara would later be copresenters at a conference at Michigan Technological University, and their theme would be losing the family farm.

At our June family gathering about the future of the Puotinen farm, we discussed my seeking a pastoral call in either Chicago, nearer to Anne and Yaz, or the Twin Cities, nearer to Sara and Scott. So in

July, I contacted the ELCA Synods in Chicago, Minneapolis, and Saint Paul. In October we also listed our farm property for sale with a local realtor as two separate forty-acre parcels. The first forty, which included our farmhouse, barn, and other buildings, sold first. The back forty, with woodland bordering the Hemlock River, sold a few weeks later. The John Flowers family bought the front forty and moved in with their horses, dogs, and cats. Long-time residents in Iron County, they brought know-how, care, and purpose, and we were heartened that they made the farm usable and sustainable once again. A daughter of the couple residing next to the back forty purchased it, so this transfer of the wooded parcel to her pleased us as well.

In retrospect, I see that it is disruptive and challenging to move and to change your life and career. Leadership requires trusting oneself, others, and God that good things do happen. Courage to unleash the lion in you creates wonderful restorative and creative powers in you to survive and thrive. Finlandia University moved forward in its vision and mission, and Judy developed a new purpose and knowledge for life as a fine arts graduate. My pastoral call at First Lutheran Church in Iron River renewed my passion to serve God and people as a parish pastor. Our family upgraded the Puotinen family farm and enjoyed its heritage and various family visits and gatherings.

Yet changing economic circumstances created a new opportunity. Like the river that ran through our farm, we needed to move on to a new place. The reality of ever-changing life is expressed by the Greek philosopher Heraclitus, who said, "No man ever steps in the same river twice, for it's not the same river and·he's not the same man." That changing river was our pool of discovery.

You Reconnect with Your Family

Share how you would feel or have felt moving to live closer to your family.

Judy and I made an exploratory trip to Chicago in August 2004 for my interview with Bishop Paul Landahl and his associates of the Metropolitan Chicago Synod of the Evangelical Lutheran Church in America. After our visit, they submitted my name to the call committee of Bethlehem Lutheran Church in Elgin, which was searching for a new pastor. After several steps in their call process, we visited the congregation in mid-November, and I agreed to begin my work in Elgin during the 2004 Christmas week. We also signed a purchase agreement on our new home in Elgin the same day, after two days of searching various home sites.

The leave-taking from Iron River was difficult. Many First Lutheran members were disappointed that we were leaving after only two years of service and just two weeks' notice. Judy packed her art supplies and our household items while my numerous tasks and concluding events at the church allowed some time to help.

A moving company from Calumet, Michigan, loaded their van with our household goods in mid-December, and off we went to Elgin on December 15. The movers unloaded our goods at our new home on December 16. I spent a few hours at the Bethlehem Lutheran Church office on December 17 and preached and led two worship services on December 19. We were warmly welcomed, and my tenth call in ministry began with a festive celebration of Christmas with me wanting to be in Bethlehem for this festival holiday.

In mid-January 2005, Judy and I went to Australia to be with Marji and Glenn, his family, and their friends for two weeks. She had a teaching position at the University of Wollongong, not far from Sydney, and he was serving in the Australian Air Force, in charge of airplane mechanics at a regional base. They were well suited for each other.

We celebrated a blessing of their marriage at a hillside resort overlooking the ocean. I officiated. Judy and Lois, Glenn's mother, released a group of Monarch butterflies in lieu of the traditional unity candle. We enjoyed being with their family and friends during the summer season down under. On Australia Day—the counterpart of the Fourth of July—the newlyweds took us to the Sydney harbor for a day of sightseeing. Marji took Judy and me for a trip into the Blue Mountains, and we cut the walking tour short because Judy lacked the energy that she used to have from walking four miles a day.

We returned to Elgin in early February 2005 for more winter, unpacking, and getting Judy's art studio in place in our spacious basement. At Bethlehem Lutheran, our team of worship leaders prepared for the Lenten season and coordinated a Wednesday evening series of worship services.

Two years at First Lutheran in Iron River had gotten me into the rhythm and flow of parish life, preparing for Sunday worship services, teaching confirmation students, visiting the hospitalized and homebound, and other responsibilities. Bethlehem offered a traditional worship service at nine and a contemporary service at ten thirty. In the first, I wore vestments and conducted worship from the *Lutheran Book of Worship* (LBW); in the second, I wore my regular suit and played the guitar for the service, consisting of modified LBW liturgy and praise songs. In both services, my preaching primarily focused on the Gospel reading for the day and its application for daily life. This style would continue and serve as the framework for later Sundays and my occasional reflections on health and healing.

That summer Judy and I flew by plane to New York City for a short vacation. It was over ninety degrees each day as we traveled by subway to museums and to shops in the garment district. Judy bought some materials there for future projects. We walked to see the former World Trade Center area—a sober remembering the Twin Towers tragedy on September 11, 2001. Our hotel was in the Battery Center overlooking the harbor and the Statue of Liberty. Overall, we enjoyed the trip.

Suggestions for Renewing Your Life and Relationships

- **Look after your physical health.** The mind and body are connected. When you feel good physically, you'll also feel better emotionally. Reduce stress and fatigue by getting enough sleep, eating right, and exercising.
- **Don't let anyone tell you how to feel, and don't tell yourself how to feel either.** Your stress is your own, and no one else can tell you when it's time to "move on" or "get over it." Let yourself feel whatever you feel without embarrassment or judgment. It's okay to be angry, to yell at the heavens, to cry or not to cry. It's also okay to laugh, to find moments of joy, and to let go when you're ready.
- **Find a support system.** Identify the people in your life who want to support you during this tough time. They will help you get your confidence back up where it should be.
- **Help others.** Volunteering or helping friends will remind you how valuable you can be. It will also force you to socialize when you may feel like secluding yourself.
- **Do some things you enjoy.** Now that you have some free time, do all the things you've always wanted to do, but never had time. You may not have another opportunity to do so for a while.

- **Connect with other job seekers**. Attending seminars or career networking events can help with your job search and remind you that you are not alone in this process.
- **Set goals for your personal life**. Make social plans with friends every week. Make a list of things you like to do but have not done in a long time. Make time for those activities. Just because you aren't working doesn't mean you can't have fun. If money is an issue, there are lots of low-cost activities. Hiking, playing games, or organizing a potluck supper are fun and inexpensive.
- **Be gentle with yourself.** Don't push too hard, but get "in the flow." Be persistent. As you work your plan, reevaluate it and make changes when necessary.

CHAPTER 12

Face Cancer with Courage

Lions are the only big cats that live in groups. Females mainly hunt for food; males fight off enemies when needed. Both are very social and affectionate with other pride members. Cubs are born in litters of one to five; they are carefully nurtured or completely neglected. In the second case, other lionesses allow the cub to suckle, despite it not being their own. Females babysit each other's cubs too, showing care and respect for each other.

Beneath their stereotypical ferocious appearance lives a soft, community-driven spirit. No wonder lions are used as metaphors to represent sporting teams, community centers, and countries alike. For example, Finland has the lion on its national coat of arms, representing the courage and strength of its people. Suomi College, now Finlandia University, has the lion as its mascot.

Your family has important stories of milestone events and defining moments that shape your family life and relationships. Here is such a time in the Puotinen family: Judy's journey with pancreatic cancer began in October 2005, and her courage in facing this major challenge drew her closer to her husband, her three daughters and their families, and her friends.

You Receive Medical News

Remember the time that you and/or a family member received the results of medical tests that brought major changes in your family.

In September 2005, I established a relationship with a family doctor. My visit with Dr. Richard Baley was a prelude of the journey to come. He was friendly, informed, and thorough. After hearing reports of my visits, Judy decided to consult with him too.

Dr. Baley completed the routine procedures of a first visit with Judy. The next day she gave blood and urine samples at the clinic in the same office building. Judy learned that the lab report concerned him, so she returned to the clinic for more tests, including X-rays of her abdominal area. After a few days, Judy was referred to a gastrointestinal specialist.

She met with Dr. Kosinski while I waited. Her look as she reentered the waiting room revealed that she'd received some bad news. We left quickly and went to our car, where she relayed the doctor's comments. His initial read of the X-ray and lab reports indicated visible signs of an obstruction at the head of the pancreas, near the bile duct and intestine. The possibility of pancreatic cancer existed, so he had directed her to schedule an ultrasound at Sherman Hospital in Elgin soon. He wanted to be truthful and had indicated that pancreatic cancer was a severe form of cancer with a limited survival rate.

We drove home to reflect on this unexpected turn of events. Preparing me for the worst, Judy told me she didn't have much time to live. She was glad we had moved to Elgin to be closer to our family and good health-care facilities. She said the Bethlehem congregation would provide care and support in her cancer journey and my ministry—a prophetic and true statement.

While she rested in her favorite chair, my heart felt it was going to break. Her grandmother had lived into her eighties, and her mother was an energetic eighty-one-year-old who could still touch her toes. Why should Judy be taken away too soon? She was only sixty-three.

You Face Your Toughest Time

Reflect on how you felt during your toughest time in life and what you did to make it through.

So many thoughts whirled around in my mind: All those moves in our marital journey. Saying hello to new homes, new jobs, and new relationships, and saying good-bye to familiar places, friends, and the faithful efforts we had made to lead and serve. Building a family of our own, watching her wisdom and strength as the mother of three talented daughters, and leaving a legacy they would cherish. For twenty-five years we worked together to become a presidential family in a Lutheran college. We enjoyed eight years of that journey, but that chapter ended. We returned to Suomi College and the Copper Country more than once, but our relationship there was severed. We journeyed to the Puotinen family farm, a special place for four generations, and it too was given up for purposes not yet fully clear or realized.

Home is where the heart is, and the prospect of losing my life partner due to cancer was especially difficult. Other setbacks in life had been opportunities for growth, transition times served a useful purpose, and moving on became a hopeful quest. But pancreatic cancer—this was a terminal journey that was not planned for or expected.

To keep going, we noted that the tests were not conclusive. The ultrasound might reveal a different diagnosis. So Judy made the appointment for an October Monday morning to do the ultrasound procedure at Sherman Hospital. The Saturday before her session seemed to be a good sign. The pain in her abdomen lessened, and it was a beautiful fall day in Elgin. My Sunday sermon was written; we could enjoy the day together. And our rest at day's end was peaceful.

But around three in the morning that Sunday, Judy began experiencing severe pain. She said we needed to go to the emergency room of Sherman Hospital. I drove her to there to be admitted. Judy explained to the doctor that arrangements for her ultrasound on Monday morning were made, but she needed to come early because of the pain. The doctor prepared the orders for her ultrasound, and I waited with Judy in one of the ER's screened waiting areas for her transfer. When nurses came for her, it was a time for action.

I drove to Bethlehem Lutheran Church, about a mile or so from Sherman Hospital, and phoned our organist to let her know that my sermon would be on the pulpit stand and a supply pastor would come to lead worship. It helped to know the congregation would be cared for. The supply pastor said that it would encourage our congregation to know that I was caring for my own spouse at that time.

Your Family Supports You

Remember several good times and tough times when your family members were there for you.

The ultrasound report confirmed the extent of her pancreatic cancer, and we scheduled a consultation with a respected local surgeon, Dr.

Raul Aron. He indicated the Whipple surgical procedure would be done and set the operation date for November 2.

We let our three daughters know about Judy's illness and pending surgery. They cared deeply for their mother, and Judy was especially proud of them. They are talented professionals, independent thinkers, and loving spouses and parents. Anne is an artist, an Art Institute of Chicago master's level graduate, and a fundraising professional for the Art Institute, Lincoln Park Zoo, and Joffrey Ballet in Chicago. Marji earned her PhD in environmental management at James Cook University, did extensive scientific research on the Great Barrier Reef, and has taught undergraduate and doctoral students in Australia. Sara received her PhD in women's studies and ethics at Emory University. She taught in her field at the University of Minnesota and currently works with her husband in their family consulting business.

Our three daughters came to Elgin the day before Judy's surgery. Sara is a writer and includes this fond memory of how the three daughters helped their mom get ready for surgery:

> The night before her big surgery, the one that would determine whether she lived (for how long?) or died (on the operating table?), my mom was scared. She really hated doctors and hospitals. And she didn't want to die. My oldest sister asked her if she would like to cuddle with her three daughters on the bed. She agreed, and together we—the three daughters and Rosie J, still in my womb—lay beside Mom. We held her as we waited, not knowing what would happen next.[23]

On November 2, 2005, I drove Judy, Marji, and Sara to Sherman Hospital to begin a decisive day for our family. Anne came from Chicago to be us. Judy checked in at the receptionist desk on the second floor around 7:30 a.m., and shortly afterward she was beckoned into a section of preoperative rooms for surgery patients, where we joined her.

A family friend, Pastor Dave Strang, walked into the room. Dave and Donna Strang have been friends since 1974, when Dave and I were deans at Suomi College. Dave held Judy's hand and gave a heartfelt prayer, requesting God's healing presence. Dave is a big guy (six three) with a resonant voice, and he conveys caring and strength. His visit helped a great deal.

A few moments later, it was time for Judy to be wheeled into the operating room, where her surgeon, Dr. Aron, would do the operation. With hugs and kisses, we sent Judy on her way.

In a surgery that lasted several hours, Dr. Aron removed the cancerous tumor. While she was in recovery, he met with my daughters and me. "She may have at most a year to live," he told us.

Anne asked, "Is it possible for me to take my mom on a trip to Paris?"

"Yes," he said, "but do it as soon as possible."

Judy's first words in the recovery room later to me were "Thank God for giving me back my life."

Our family rejoiced that Judy had survived the surgical procedure and recuperated enough that she could enjoy Christmas celebrations at home with us. Three daughters, three sons-in-law, and three grandchildren gathering around our table with us made it a special Christmas.

> *You Plan a Special Trip*
>
> Discuss with someone you love where they would like to go for
> a once-in-a-lifetime trip, and then make a preliminary plan for
> travel, lodging, meals, itinerary, and costs.

Anne began plans for a special trip to Paris after Judy completed
six months of chemotherapy. Meanwhile, on Fridays, my day off
as pastor, Judy and I met with Dr. Chilkamarri Yeshwant, her
oncologist. The experience of meeting in the waiting room with
other patients and family members and then going into the larger
room for her chemotherapy made a lasting impression. It was like
the Gospel story in which ill people gathered at the pool of Bethesda.
The angels here were the nurses who did the procedures and cared
for each patient.

Judy sat in a soft easy chair for an hour or more as the chemo flowed
into her body. In addition to their compassion, competence, and care,
the health-care team brought healing words. "Just remember," Dr.
Yeshwant said, "what happened to you is not because of something
you did or didn't do." It was a word of grace that we needed and
remembered when we asked why this happened to Judy. He also
encouraged Judy to travel to Paris. During this six-month regimen
of chemotherapy, consisting of three Friday mornings a month for
one and a half hours, Judy's spirit and stamina were strong.

On March 29, Sara and Scott became parents for the second time.
Baby Rosemary Judith Puotinen was born on the same birthday
as her three-year-old brother, Fletcher. It was a great boost for
Judy to hold her namesake, Rosemary Judith, a few weeks later in
Minneapolis.

In late May, Judy's oncologist, Dr. Yeshwant, decided she should have a CAT scan. On June 2, six months after her surgery, he told her there was not a trace of cancer in her body. It was wonderful news and a great blessing. We felt God's healing presence and the thoughts and prayers of many people supporting Judy in her journey. The morning Dr. Yeshwant met us, he told her the chemotherapy was complete. She was free to go, except for monthly check-ins, to enjoy life as a cancer survivor.

So in early September 2006, Judy went with Anne to Paris. In the preceding months, Anne had planned, made arrangements, and raised the funds for that memorable trip. Judy was an artist and weaver, so they planned to see beautiful art in Paris and visit the silk weavers in nearby Lyon. Marji joined them, too, as part of her travel to attend a Paris conference for her university. The pictures of these travelers reveal a happy Mom with her two daughters, enjoying a special journey.

Months after their return, Judy's pancreatic cancer came back. Another cycle of chemotherapy followed to improve her health to the extent that she was able to travel to Sydney, Australia, for the birth of Marji and Glenn's daughter April on April 29, 2007. I accompanied Judy on the long flight and returned to Elgin a week later to resume my pastoral responsibilities. Nana Judy stayed with April, Marji, and Glenn for an additional week or two, and then she expressed a desire to return home. So I went to Australia to accompany her on the return flight, which took eighteen hours. She had been courageous in making this journey to witness the birth of April and experience new joy.

Living with cancer is a reality known as the "new normal." After two overseas trips in two years that gave her joy and family fulfillment, Judy's next phase became a weekly schedule of limited activities. On Sundays she remained at home while I conducted worship services at Bethlehem. Her fiber art and weaving projects were her creative activity many mornings. Daytime TV programs and Turner Classic Movies became regular fare.

Wonderful Wednesdays became a set time for visits from long-time friend Donna Strang. Her husband, Dave, and I had lunch out together every other week, and his caring for this caregiver was welcomed and helpful. Frequent phone calls from our daughters and occasional visits by them and their families lifted Judy's spirit. A weeklong visit from her sister in Florida, Pat McKenna, also enriched Judy's life. And there were "frequent Fridays" when chemotherapy treatment with Dr. Yeshwant and staff took place, followed by luncheon and shopping for food at Woodman's store. Birthday and holiday celebrations were special joys in our life together and with family and friends.

As her pancreatic cancer and pain increased, Judy did not openly complain in public or at home. The loss of bodily control is often difficult for independent-minded people, yet she graciously accepted assistance from professional caregivers and family members and made many adjustments. She went for medical appointments and endured hospitalization, but her desire was to be at home. I adjusted my work schedule to be with her as much as possible, and in time we contracted with Sherman home health care to have various staff members provide home assistance for Judy in my absence. We juggled their four-hour shifts with my home care for her.

One day, an aide phoned me at work to tell me that Judy had fallen at home and was injured. I took her to the emergency room at Sherman Hospital. In consultation with Dr. Yeshwant, he indicated that further chemotherapy was no longer effective and adjustments were needed at home. She needed to have a hospital bed in our family room, with limited walking using a walker on that floor.

We brought our second-floor bedroom bed into the nearby living room to make me more accessible for Judy. The Sherman home care staff took turns in the morning and afternoon to provide care for Judy in my absence at work. This service was greatly needed and appreciated but not covered by health insurance. However, at a Christmas Eve service, the Bethlehem congregation surprised me during the announcements when they presented a $5,000 cash gift to help with health-care expenses. Every week the women's group at Bethlehem, known as the Rebecca Circle, took turns bringing a hot meal for Judy and serving it with their warm friendship and support.

You Begin the Final Journey

Suppose a family member or friend begins receiving hospice care; identify several things to do and say that could be helpful to that person.

The next phase in Judy's illness occurred when Dr. Yeshwant advised us to secure the assistance of St. Joseph Hospice services. Twice a week, a registered nurse monitored her vital signs, pain medications, bandages for her bedsores, and took other measures to keep her safe and comfortable. A social worker talked weekly with Judy and me to assess how she was responding to the new situation and provided written and verbal information on adjusting to the final stages of life. The chaplain offered prayer and spiritual insights to us. Having lost his first wife to cancer, he understood what we were going through.

A boyhood experience helped me know what was needed. My grandparents, Elias and Johanna, had spent their final days at our family farm in Michigan with my parents, Kully and Ines, providing round-the-clock care for them in their illnesses. In my mind's eye, I remembered Elias lying in a bed in the living room during his final weeks of life. Years later, when Johanna began this final phase, her first-floor bedroom was near the living room. Often I overheard her saying aloud the Lord's Prayer and Apostles' Creed to find comfort in her illness.

At home with Judy, our life together meant caregiving at a new level. The situation required me to prepare food, to serve meals, to wash dishes and clothes, and to do other chores. My role was to be her male nurse, at times in essential ways, such as providing medication, changing bedding and bandages, and responding to immediate needs.

Although Judy lost weight and physical strength, her strong spirit and resolve remained. I read her scripture and said prayers. She rarely if ever complained, and being in her presence gave family members and caregivers a blessing.

Life with cancer is a journey to receive each day as a gift, to persist in each struggle and suffering, and to fulfill your promise from God. Her love for each family member enabled us to live with her cancer and to accept both the highs and the lows of that journey.

Judy's experiences helped me also in my ministry. On Sundays I would go to Bethlehem to preach the good news of Jesus Christ, while a Sherman home health staff member stayed with Judy. My prayer often was, "Good Lord, we need your healing power. Give us strength to carry on, to do God's work, and to give comfort to Judy in her life with us."

We were blessed to have a caring congregation, family, and friends. Our journey with cancer became a point of connection with members and others that were experiencing health struggles of their own. People would tell me, "You understand what we're going through," and they welcomed my visits and prayers for God's healing power and comfort for their loved ones. The Twenty-Third Psalm and other biblical passages were well received. Two favorite Bible verses lifted me: the Apostle Paul wrote, "The power of God to raise Jesus from the dead is alive and at work in you," and "I can do all things through Christ who strengthens me."

These pastoral experiences ranged from officiating at the wedding of a pancreatic cancer survivor to doing memorial services for men and women who died because of cancer. A young married couple was saddened by the stillborn death of their first child, but they were gladdened at the baptism of their next child. Many poignant memories of other families that suffered come to mind, and my life with Judy and her cancer helped me be a better, more caring pastor for others.

The hospice team helped in many ways. The hands-on health care by the nurses relieved pain and prolonged Judy's life. They also helped us deal with the inevitable reality of her pending death. I asked, "When will be her time to leave us?" The nurse replied, "It's up to her and God. In the meantime it's important that you talk with her and tell her that it is okay for her to leave you." The social worker said, "Judy has fought the good fight for so long to help you face and accept her death when it happens and to move ahead to a new phase in your life."

Saying good-bye to Judy became an extended conversation. Our daughters came from their homes to have such a talk, and they did it in memorable fashion. Anne prepared a gourmet meal for them to share with their mom, Marji told stories, and Sara provided entertainment with her solos of songs from the Broadway show, *The Sound of Music.*

The weekly visits by the nurses continued as Judy's health wavered between temporary improvement and impending death. Dr. Yeshwant came for a home visit with Judy to give his blessing. Pastor

Dave and his wife, Donna, said good-bye to her with prayer and hugs. My last-rite prayers were said several times as she sometimes alternated between final breaths and fresh energy.

The final time did come in a memorable way. The signs were there that Judy would pass before too long. Marji made flight arrangements to come from Australia, and Anne went from Chicago to meet her sister at O'Hare Airport and then drive to our home. Judy waited to see them once more for a final good-bye that evening. Anne then returned home, Marji went to sleep after her long flight, and I stayed up with Judy until around eleven o'clock.

Periodically during the night I awakened to check on her, and around four in the morning on September 29, 2010, she died. A hospice nurse came and confirmed her passing. Laird Funeral Home of Elgin dispatched two staff members to come for Judy's body prior to its cremation per her request. Now her earthly life with cancer was over, and the promise of eternal life Jesus expressed in the Gospel of John 14:1–6 to those who have faith in God became our hope and comfort too.

> *You Plan a Memorial Service*
>
> Take time with a loved one to discuss how he or she wants to be celebrated, and then honor that request.

A memorial service to celebrate Judy's life, to comfort our grieving family and friends, and to hear the biblical words concerning Christ's resurrection and eternal life focused our efforts in the days that followed. Anne, Marji, and Sara prepared a video presentation honoring Judy, and her signature woven kimonos that depicted her roles in life (mother and grandmother, teacher, student artist, and president's spouse) adorned the chancel area. Pastor Dave gave the homily; I read the service liturgy. The assembled congregation included Judy's family, Bethlehem members and community friends, and our ELCA bishop, Wayne Miller.

During Judy's four-year journey with cancer, we had shared joys and sorrows, focused on daily health-care procedures and practices, and thought often of our family and her future. We updated our wills, signed do-not-resuscitate paperwork, and planned our funerals to include cremation and placement of our ashes at the Puotinen family burial plot in the Amasa cemetery.

Judy's courage in facing each day with diminishing physical strength did not lessen her love and concern for her family and friends. I felt her spirit and desire to support me in my ministry at Bethlehem, and she gave me her blessing to begin a new life when she left us to be with the Lord in heaven. Faith in the resurrection to eternal life through Jesus Christ offers comfort in grieving the death of a love one and provides courage to resume life and relationships.

The celebration of Judy's life continued into the following weeks. I assembled the kimonos and video presentation and made a trip to Grand View College in Des Moines, where I gave the program to members of the college community, including President Kent Henning, members of the board of trustees, administration and faculty, students and community members. Several years later, a new memorial brick garden on the Grand View campus included a brick for Judy Puotinen, for the parents of President Henning, and for several others in the college community. Creative and courageous Judy Puotinen had unleashed her lion to enrich the lives of people she inspired and cared for.

Suggestions for Caring during the Cancer Journey

- **Meet with the patient's doctor** to determine when the advanced stages of cancer are approaching. If home care is possible, obtain necessary medical equipment and make necessary adjustments.

- **Place books, a stereo, and/or a TV** and VCR or DVD player within easy reach of the patient's bed or chair.

- **Be informed.** Have, at minimum, a basic working understanding of the medical mechanisms at work in cancer and its prognosis. MayoClinic.com is an excellent online resource.

- **Communicate often with your afflicted friend or family member.** Make daily inquiries to see if there are any simple items she needs or if there are any basic things you can do to improve her comfort.

- **Check with the patient's life insurance or long-term care insurance policies** to see if she qualifies for any benefits during her period of hospice care.

- **Hire a home-care nurse or assistant.** Cancer patients, especially as their condition intensifies, require daily, qualified medical attention.

- **Arrange for someone from your local Meals on Wheels or other food service to deliver a meal** if you have to be away from the patient during the day.

- **Contact your local social services bureau** to see if the patient qualifies for a social worker or someone that can assist with practical tasks, such as laundering linens or sitting with the patient for a few hours or overnight.

- **Spread the workload.** Whenever possible, enlist the help of the patient's friends and family members to provide you with occasional relief of your caregiving.

- **Take a leave of absence from your job,** if possible, to care for your loved one and care for your own well-being.
- **Plan ahead for grief "triggers."** Anniversaries, holidays, and milestones can reawaken memories and feelings. Be prepared for an emotional wallop, and know that it's completely normal. If you're sharing a holiday or lifecycle event with other relatives, talk to them ahead of time about their expectations, and agree on strategies to honor the person you love.

CHAPTER 13

You Can Love Again

Being left alone was graphically conveyed by a widow friend who quietly said to me, "What are you going to do with the hole in your heart?" Life without your partner is also expressed in the lyrics to "The Lion in the Winter" by Hoyt Axton. His duet with Linda Ronstadt portrays a lonely lion longing for its departed mate in colder nights and remembering her call in warmer days.

The death of a spouse is the most stressful and traumatic experience a person can endure. While it's normal to feel lonely after a spouse's death, it's also important to take steps to avoid isolation and reclaim your happiness. Isolation was not my option, as I chose to continue my pastoral responsibilities at Bethlehem Lutheran Church and community activities. My family and friends became powerful sources of strength and encouragement. My spiritual reading and meditation brought me back from a feeling of lack to thoughts of abundance and gratitude. Caring for and counseling congregational members became therapeutic for them and me.

Conventional wisdom is that after the death of a spouse you should wait a year or so before making any major life changes. The grief process generally takes time, and financial and other adjustments are necessary. Widowers respond to the death of their wife in various ways. Our hospice chaplain lost his wife due to cancer, took some time off, and climbed the Alps before returning to work. Another friend gave extended care to his dear wife with terminal brain cancer and waited a year before making household changes and dating a female friend.

My grief process went through several stages:

- Shock that Judy had pancreatic cancer and that it was terminal
- Surgery and recovery, and her thankfulness for new life
- Sustained chemotherapy and our adjustments to the "new normal" lifestyle
- Season of joy in her being cancer-free and her travel to Paris, enjoyment of the birth of new grandchildren, and of the love and support from family and friends
- Sadness at the return of pancreatic cancer and her year at home with hospice care
- Seeking closure of final life plans through family discussions, financial arrangements, final good-byes, and preparations
- Standing in hope and faith in God's promise of the resurrection from the dead

For four years, God blessed Judy, me, and our family with the opportunity to grieve periodically, love continually, and hope expectantly for the life to come.

A month after Judy's memorial service, several friends started encouraging me to date someone. Maybe they understood me and knew that grieving has a timetable that varies depending on the circumstance and the one grieving. A high school classmate and his wife invited me to supper with our widowed classmate. I also received encouragement to share a date with a church member, but received it with caution, because ELCA church policies include certain boundaries regarding pastors dating their congregational members and entering into long-term relationships.

You Begin the Dating Game

Ask a few people what a single older adult should do to find new friends, and begin dating once again.

Believing it wise to find such a friend elsewhere than the Bethlehem congregation, I initially enrolled with eHarmony, an online dating website designed to match single men and women for long-term relationships. The company compiles a profile of each person's characteristics, preferences, and other information. It was helpful to complete this process, which clarifies values and expectations.

Before long I began sending and receiving e-mails with information about potential dating partners, followed by exchanges of written responses. One woman wrote that widowers with a happy marriage often were more ready to enter into a serious relationship. She understood me. I was open to finding a new mate, rather than just have a date. She wrote that she had just started a new business with several friends and needed to wait a few months before meeting me in person.

In the meantime, I continued my pastoral responsibilities, and my private prayers included a petition for God's help and direction to begin a new life. At Bethlehem Church, we began an online Bible study that twenty people came to weekly. Several members wanted to meet as a small group on Saturday mornings for fellowship and discussion of the weekly lesson of one of the epistles or letters of the Apostle Paul. I led the lively discussions.

Carol Schaley of Elgin participated in that Bible study group. She served on the Bethlehem Church Council that had called me to be the new pastor. One of my first pastoral acts in 2005 was to officiate at the marriage of her son, Brin Schaley, and Maria Perez. They met with me to plan their wedding, a beautiful outdoor ceremony at Villa Olivia in August 2005. Customary contacts between pastor and members, such as worship services, committee meetings, Bible studies, and other events, were a prelude for Carol and my later relationship. She also encouraged us with her provision of several meals during Judy's cancer journey and her gift to Judy of a painting of a beautiful rose.

Knowing Carol's long-standing artistic abilities, I invited her to accompany me for a day trip to the Art Institute in Chicago in mid-January of 2010. She agreed to do so, believing that this time together was a thank-you for her friendship. Our trip included conversation on the Metra train, in the art galleries, and over lunch. We talked about mutual interests and our families.

Carol is a talented artist who studied at the Art Institute of Chicago, the graphic design program at Elgin Community College, and the Botanical Art School of the Morton Arboretum in Lisle, Illinois. Her specialty in botanical illustration in a variety of mediums led to her exhibiting numerous paintings in local and regional venues.

An active member of Bethlehem Lutheran Church, Carol joined the congregation in 1988 with her late husband. She has served on the church council and several committees for many years, sings alto in the church choir, and attends worship regularly. Her husband Ed Schaley passed away unexpectedly while cross country skiing in 2000, leaving his immediate survivors: Carol, their four adult children, Evin, Brin, Joel, and Kera, and other family members.

Widowed for ten years, Carol had transitioned into a new independent lifestyle. She sold the vintage Elgin home that she, Ed, and their sons had renovated, and she moved into a townhome overlooking a lake not far from Bethlehem Lutheran Church and downtown Elgin. Her family members gathered in her new place for holiday celebrations and meals.

Carol enjoyed concerts of the Elgin Symphony Orchestra, and she served as an orchestra board member during her two years as president of the Elgin Symphony League of volunteers. She made several overseas travel tours with ESO friends that were fundraisers for the symphony. She traveled with her stepmother, Florence Kucharik, and helped her with her life transitions. Carol continued her active membership at Bethlehem Lutheran, the local Art for All artist group, and the Morton Arboretum Nature Artists' Guild. She volunteered at PADS (the Public Action to Deliver Shelter), the Soup Kitchen, and other social service agencies. Having reached a greater degree of independence and a sustainable lifestyle, Carol had not expected to find a new life partner.

Then, in late January of 2010, Carol and my relationship began to blossom. We went out for coffee after choir practice a couple of times, and her friend Joan Hanover accompanied us on a dinner date as a "chaperone." In early February of 2010, the Lutheran Educational Conference of North America invited me to attend their centennial anniversary meeting in Florida. Many LECNA college and university presidents and their spouses remembered me and Judy from earlier days, and they were interested to know more about Judy and my current activities. They were excited and encouraging to know about my pastorate at Bethlehem Lutheran and my new relationship with Carol.

Being apart for a few days confirmed our growing attraction for each other. After my return to Elgin, Carol and I began letting her four children and my three children know about our developing relationship. Kera was pleased, for she had encouraged her mother to get better acquainted with me, even though Carol initially said I was not her type. Her three sons were fine with the growing friendship and hoped their mother would be well cared for.

My three daughters had lost their beloved mother just four months before, so we needed to be sensitive in our disclosure. We invited Anne and Yaz and their children, Isabel and Sylvia, to my home for dinner. Carol prepared the meal at her home and brought over the food. The visit went well, and Carol returned home so I could visit with the others. My question about how things went and what they felt about Carol was answered by granddaughters Isabel and Sylvia giving me two thumbs up.

Meeting face-to-face with Marji, living in Australia, and Sara, living in Minneapolis, presented a challenge because of the distance. Fortunately Marji had a flight to the United States for a conference, with a stopover in Minneapolis with Sara and family. I booked a flight for the Twin Cities so I could have a meal with them on that Valentine's Day weekend and reveal my fondness for Carol and our desire to move ahead together. Memories of their mom remained strong, yet they wanted their dad to be happy.

When I returned to Elgin the next day, I gifted Carol with a friendship ring and subsequently informed the Bethlehem Lutheran Church Council and Bishop Wayne Miller that—in the language of my high school days—"We're going steady now." We were transparent with family, friends, and church leaders in our newly found joy. We honored the ELCA church policy regarding committed relationships between a pastor and church member. In doing so, Carol and I received their blessing and began discussing when to get married.

> *You Plan a Family Wedding*
>
> Remember a wedding in your family and how the bride and groom involve family members and friends in appropriate ways in the marriage ceremony.

We chose July 3, 2010, for our wedding to be held at Bethlehem Lutheran Church with Pastor Dave officiating. Carol's daughter, Kera, agreed to be maid of honor, and my son-in-law Yazid became my best man. The bridal party included other family members as musicians, lectors, flower girls, and a ring bearer. Bethlehem organist Peg Youngren and four high school youths as ushers completed the cast for the ceremony. Wedding guests included an array of members from our families and congregation as well as community friends and other loved ones.

In many respects, our wedding was traditional. There was a good crowd, beautiful music on a sunny day, and a message from Dave with memorable counsel. He proclaimed, "Everyone here knows and you know that you have experienced being married for many years. Likewise everyone here knows and you will know soon that when you get married now, you will have adjustments to make."

> *You Make Adjustments*
>
> Identify the top three adjustments you face in starting a new relationship or marriage.

Carol added some creative touches to the ceremony. Her three sons took turns escorting her up the aisle. She composed our wedding vows, and I liked what she wrote, so we pledged the vows from memory without a single slip during the service. I had seen a YouTube video of a wedding in Minneapolis in which an exuberant wedding party danced up the aisle as the wedding began. My suggestion was that we dance down the aisle together, so we included some festive steps as part of the recessional. Peg Youngren played an up-tempo gospel song, and Carol and I danced down the aisle. Carol also arranged for a string quartet from the Elgin Symphony Orchestra to provide music during the festive meal and the first dance of the newlyweds at the wedding reception at the Villa Olivia Country Club.

The next day being July Fourth, Carol and I hosted a picnic at my home in west Elgin for members of both families. It was a joyous time with food, family, and fellowship before many returned home and we prepared for our honeymoon trip. Going forward as a couple, we were Dad and Carol to the Puotinen family and Mom and Art to the Schaley family.

Carol's friends Ralph and Jeanne Forest had a time-share for a week in Kauai, Hawaii, and they invited us to stay in their lockout room as a wedding gift. We enjoyed their company, the accommodations, and the day trips so much that we agreed to join them the following year for a river cruise from Paris to Normandy Beach, with three additional days in Paris.

We newlyweds returned home from our Hawaii honeymoon early on a Saturday morning to prepare for Sunday worship and the weekly pastoral schedule as we began our new life together. Then, on August 9, Carol's son Evin and his wife, Mary Jo Schmer, were united in marriage on the Chicago Odyssey Cruise Ship on Navy Pier with me officiating. All aboard enjoyed the dinner cruise and toasted the newlywed couple.

You Move into a New Home

Before moving to a new place, identify several items you need and several items you can donate and/or discard.

Prior to our festive wedding, Carol and I faced a practical issue: Where would we live? Carol had an attractive, two-story townhome in Elgin with a water view in the back, and my two-story colonial home had a basement that housed Judy's artist studio. We decided to sell both homes in April and buy a different one to begin anew in our forthcoming marriage. We listed both properties with local realtors, and Carol succeeded in selling her home.

My situation required some adjustments in order to qualify for purchasing our new home. The 2010 economic downturn had depressed the market, and my home needed a new roof, new appliances, and new carpeting to compete. I lowered the sale price and offered the home for sale or lease with an option to buy. With her townhome sale and a signed sale or lease agreement on my property, we would qualify for a mortgage on the new home.

This price change with options increased interest, and several bidders came forward in late June. One bidder offered to buy my home, requiring a move-in date by July 15. I accepted the offer, creating considerable stress for Carol and me as we needed to pack and store household belongings before that due date. Just prior to our wedding on July 3, the bidder backed out of the contract. We had no contract, but by the time our honeymoon ended, our realtor had several potential bidders for the lease option.

We newlyweds returned from our Hawaii honeymoon early on a Saturday morning to meet with our realtor for negotiations with five families interested in my property. In the next few days we had face-to-face interviews with five married couples seeking the lease-to-own option on our Elgin property. This experience opened our eyes to the financial challenges families face in uncertain economic times. Finally we entered into a three-year lease contract with a family of four that began August 1.

The signed lease with option to buy along with the sale of Carol's townhome enabled us to qualify for a new home and mortgage in Elgin. We moved into our new place on September 1 with help from various people. Some Bethlehem church members, Carol's son Joel Schaley, and we worked together to stage my home for sale, to pack our belongings from both houses, and assist a local moving company in the transfer of household items into our new home. The new house had room enough to contain everything.

September was a busy time at Bethlehem Church with the start-up of fall programs, regular worship, and committee meetings. The next chapter details the exciting partnership of Bethlehem and San Esteban Martir congregations that added to our ministry activities. While I mainly focused on these events, Carol led in such projects as unpacking boxes, arranging furniture, and otherwise settling the house for entertaining family, Bethlehem groups, and other friends during holiday gatherings in our new home. We hosted and enjoyed many events in the coming months. It was an exciting time to begin our new life together.

Suggestions for Dating and Finding a Mate

- **Find the right partner.** Try an online dating service, or begin having coffee or lunch with someone you already know. Make an effort to find out early if you share common interests, values, likes, and dislikes.
- **Be patient and take your time.** The potential partner may not be ready to form new ties or jump into a love

relationship. Sometimes being a supportive friend is a good idea, at least in the beginning.

- **Talk about your deceased spouse** without going overboard. Your late husband or wife continues to be part of your life experiences, and sharing stories with the new person strengthens that budding relationship.
- **Use your best manners.** Etiquette is important when you are getting to know someone, which is easy for widowed singles to forget, because they lived with their spouses long enough to have stopped common courtesies, such as holding doors or pulling out chairs.
- **Put their needs first and enjoy the moment when you start to fall in love again.** Mark the occasion. Tell your family and receive their blessing. Make plans for your future life together.
- **Remember that you have adjustments to make,** and your many acts of loving-kindness for your partner will make it better. Amen!

CHAPTER 14

Lead Together in Mission

Suppose there were two little lions in the field with the sheep, and the big lion taught them both to roar. Then he brought them to the pool of water to discover who they were and what they could do together.

A TV production film crew went into the African wild and recorded a story of two lion cub brothers. This true story depicted how these young males lived and worked together to build their own pride, defend one another in fights with rival lions, and get along with the females and cubs in their extended pride.

This lion story offers an example for human leaders. Competition and rivalry often occur within and between organizations as individuals seek to be in the forefront or at the top of their field. It happens in church life too, as pastors of different congregations seek new members from residents in the same community, offering similar services and programs, while meeting the spiritual needs of members and newcomers.

What if two brothers in Jesus Christ decided to work together and help one another and their respective flocks in a new venture to grow their faith communities? Unleashed with the Spirit's power, two pastors can have a new partnership in ministry in Elgin with the people of their congregations.

You Brainstorm Together

Take a moment to brainstorm a potential project, joint venture, or partnership that you and another leader can do to make good things happen.

Early in 2008, Pastor Antonio Cabello of San Esteban Martir, or St. Stephen's Lutheran Church, of Carpentersville—a town five miles north of Bethlehem Lutheran Church—began having informal conversations with me. He noted that some San Esteban Martir members and other prospective members lived in Elgin—a city of over one hundred thousand residents, including 40 percent of Hispanic background. As an outreach of San Esteban Martir, he proposed offering a Christian education hour on Saturdays followed by a worship service at noon at our church site. He also felt that a community-based early childhood ministry underway at Bethlehem could benefit San Esteban families.

The Child Development Center (CDC) began as a ministry of Bethlehem Lutheran and celebrates its twentieth anniversary in 2015. In two decades of early childhood education and day care in the greater Elgin area, the CDC has welcomed children that range from toddlers to kindergarten students. Currently eleven full-time staff members are serving seventy students Monday through Friday from 6:30 a.m. to 6:00 p.m. in the Bethlehem Church's facilities. Students and their families represent a diversity of ethnic, economic, and educational backgrounds. Kelly Aurand, the CDC director, began her work at CDC in 2006. The teachers are dedicated in length of service, have creative teaching methods, and care for each student. Together they represent a long-term commitment and involvement to this ministry. The CDC board of directors includes Bethlehem members and family representatives. The Illinois Department of Child and Family Services certifies the CDC.

Several funding sources underwrite the CDC program, and parents provide tuition payments for many students. The State of Illinois pays tuition for some students based on their family's economic need. Bethlehem Lutheran provides rent-free facilities, funding for projects, and other institutional support. Grand Victoria Foundation has awarded the CDC grant funds for eight years for operating costs and special projects based on competitive proposal requests. The first grant followed a strategic planning process by a CDC task force of church members, teachers, and staff. Aurand worked with me to prepare and present the successful grant proposals. Other smaller fundraisers occur in the fall and spring. The State of Illinois budget crisis in recent years may impact the future tuition funding for some CDC students and families.

Pastor Antonio and I talked to members of both congregations about working together and then sought a mission grant from the Metropolitan Chicago Synod ELCA for the proposed Saturday ministry at the Bethlehem site. After receiving approval of the grant, we pastors requested and received final approval by both congregations to proceed with the Saturday program of San Esteban Martir at Bethlehem Lutheran Church.

Our partnership in ministry began in the spring of 2009, and the bilingual ministry on Saturday mornings in English and Spanish continued at Bethlehem Church for two years. We also developed several combined congregational events, such as Thanksgiving Eve worship, the Feast of Guadalupe, a Santa Lucia worship service, and other fellowship experiences.

After extended reflection by its members, San Esteban Martir decided to sell its church property in Carpentersville in the fall of 2010 and to discern the place and shape of its future ministry. They requested and received approval to worship in our Bethlehem Lutheran church building while exploring where to relocate their congregation. The Bethlehem Church Council agreed to welcome San Esteban members to worship in the Bethlehem sanctuary at noon on Sundays and invite their children into our Sunday school program. Combined Lenten weekday, Holy Week, and Easter worship services also took place.

This pattern and practice of ministry together at the Bethlehem Lutheran church site resulted in several outcomes. St. Stephen's developed a long-term partnership with Bethlehem Church. Initial conversations among representatives from both church councils affirmed "the principle that our two congregations continue to exist separately and work cooperatively in mutual ministry for our current and future members in the greater Elgin area." Both congregations in their annual meetings in January, 2011 adopted this working principle.

At its July meeting, the Bethlehem Church Council agreed to extend the working agreement with St. Stephen's for the remainder of 2011 with the understanding that further exploration and long-term planning would take place. The Cooperative Ministries Committee (CMC), with pastors and lay leaders from both congregations, was formed. We began to meet monthly to work separately and together in fulfilling the commission of Jesus Christ to be his disciples. We focused on developing a five-year Partnership Planning Process for presentation to both church councils and congregations on June 10, 2012. They authorized the continuation of the planning efforts. Focus-group meetings in both congregations were helpful in the planning process. A positive attitude and welcoming spirit became evident in both congregations regarding our partnership in ministry.

The Koinonia Leadership Project provided additional impetus for building the partnership of the two congregations. Pastor Antonio and I, five members from Bethlehem, and one member from San Esteban participated in the Koinonia Leadership program. It involved thirty hours of training over several weekends for twelve ELCA Lutheran congregations in Chicagoland. Funded by the Metro Chicago Synod and participating congregations, this two-year program in transformational leadership in the local parish was developed and taught by leaders of Stephen Ministries of Saint Louis, Missouri. Our Koinonia team members led a Bethlehem process of reaffirming core values of the congregation, restating its mission, and refining its vision to include the Hispanic congregation in future planning.

You Develop Other Leaders

Describe a planning process you used to develop leaders in your family, business, or organization.

The 9:00 a.m. traditional worship at Bethlehem Lutheran included children, youths, and parents for the first part of the service before going on to Sunday school and youth group sessions. Thereafter, the coffee fellowship, the 10:30 contemporary worship, and a noon bilingual service took place until Pastor Antonio accepted a new call in Madison, Wisconsin. Both congregations combined for bilingual midweek worship during Lent and Holy Week, Reformation Sunday, and Thanksgiving Eve. Both pastors worked together in the sacraments of baptism and Holy Communion, as well as rites of affirmation of baptism, weddings, and funerals. Also, we provided pulpit supply when the other pastor was away.

Combining children and youth from both congregations in Sunday school and youth group on Sunday morning increased numbers in both programs, created more of a church family feeling in worship, and allowed for special messages for children and youth.

In December, the Swedish tradition Sancta Lucia Festival of Light and Supper of Bethlehem welcomed 160 participants, and the Mexican tradition of the San Esteban Festival of Guadalupe attracted ninety. Both congregations gathered on Sunday mornings during the coffee hour and at the annual church picnic in July.

Cooperative Ministry Committee members led efforts to upgrade external signage and to create the Trinity Chapel in the Bethlehem sanctuary overflow area with liturgical artifacts from the San Esteban congregation. Community service volunteers assisted with landscaping improvements.

The annual Bethlehem Strawberry Festival during the first week of May 2012, in which both congregations participated, received an Elgin Image Award that produced grant funds for several local social service organizations and congregational missions. Other partnership activities included soup kitchen assistance and food drives.

You Progress through Partnership

List and celebrate the good results from your partnership within your group and with other groups.

The San Esteban Martir congregation provided financial support to Bethlehem for property usage and other expenses and agreed to do so again in 2013. The pattern of partnership continued for the remainder of the year, and then a new dynamic entered the situation. I retired from Bethlehem Lutheran Church in June 2013, and Pastor Antonio accepted a call to a new pastoral position in Madison, beginning in January 2014. Supply pastors began covering the noon bilingual service while other cooperative ministries of the two congregations continued. Interim Pastor Paul Olson came to Bethlehem in August 2013 and began serving members of both congregations in worship, Christian education, and other activities.

Members of San Esteban Martir discussed their future as a congregation among themselves and with staff members of the Metropolitan Chicago Synod. In January 2014, they voted to discontinue their congregation and to encourage members to join Bethlehem. Many families had enrolled their children in the Bethlehem Sunday school, confirmation, or youth ministry and valued the welcome they had experienced.

San Esteban Martir members requested that their archival material concerning the legacy of their church be housed at Bethlehem and that any remaining San Esteban funds be placed in a fund named San Esteban Spanish Outreach Ministry.

On April 20, 2014, Easter Sunday, San Esteban held its final worship service at noon, and on Sunday, April 27, Bishop Wayne Miller of the Metropolitan Chicago Synod preached at the 9:00 and 10:30 services at Bethlehem. He led a Closing Liturgy for the Dissolution of a Congregation at the end of each service and gave thanks for the Gospel witness of San Esteban Martir over the years.

There were several reasons for sadness at this event: the dissolution of a bilingual Hispanic congregation in a growing Hispanic community, the limited availability of bilingual pastors to serve San Esteban Martir, the departure of dynamic Pastor Antonio Cabello, and other organizational factors that influenced the decision.

The affirmation of gladness at this event also had several dimensions. The vision of partnership in ministry linking San Esteban Martir and Bethlehem Lutheran had born fruit in its welcoming spirit, the inclusion of youth from both congregations in cooperative Christian education experiences, and the preservation of Hispanic culture and ministry in the fund for the San Esteban Spanish Outreach Ministry.

The ongoing partnership is bearing fruit. A score and more San Esteban youth received their first communion at Bethlehem, completed two years of instruction leading to the Rite of Confirmation, and participated in the July 2014 youth-group mission trip to Cincinnati. Two adult members from San Esteban joined the Bethlehem Church Council in July and more than twenty family members became Bethlehem members. The future of the partnership is open for development by the members of both congregations with new pastoral leadership. Pastor Paul Olson served as interim pastor of Bethlehem Lutheran Church for eighteen months.

The Pastoral Search Committee completed its work and recommended to the church council and the Annual Meeting of Bethlehem Lutheran Church that a new pastor be called to serve. On January 25, 2015, the Rev. Carol Book was elected, and she began her ministry in March of 2015. She is a fluent bilingual speaker with other attributes that commend her for the blended congregation at Bethlehem.

You Face a Turnover in Leadership

Indicate what happens in your organization when leaders leave and how new leaders and members step forward to continue the mission.

When I reflect on my eight and a half years as pastor of Bethlehem, I especially remember that many good people worked together to make good things happen. Its members and friends responded to my pastoral care by caring for and supporting one another and my family, just as Judy predicted. The new partnership with San Esteban required vision, work, and courage from everyone. Delaying my retirement from Bethlehem until reaching age seventy-two provided continuity in forming the partnership in ministry. Leadership by members in both congregations was essential, as was the cooperative approach between Pastor Antonio and me. We enjoyed working together. In my last Sunday leading worship, June 1, 2013, my signature sermon, "There's a Lion in You," encouraged our friends to be courageous brothers and sisters in Jesus Christ. New blessings at Bethlehem are now happening.

Suggestions on Being Partners in Mission

The Bethlehem–San Esteban Martir partnership occurred because leaders and members of both congregations chose to do the following:

- Share common views on faith and doctrine
- Respect the culture and heritage of each partner congregation
- Agree on governance and leadership in the church partnership
- Determine the plan for use of church property and financial responsibilities
- Build relationships among both congregations with a common church mission and vision
- Prepare pastoral and lay leaders for the organization and participation in shared activities
- Work together during pastoral transitions
- Develop a planning and budgeting process for the partnership activities that was approved and monitored by both congregations
- Keep church communications open, frequent, and flexible among the partner congregations

- Vote as church members on major decisions to bring everyone on board. Having a process to discuss and debate with members can be culturally healthy and worth the time invested.
- Use your church building, grounds, and signage efficiently to promote the partnership of both congregations.
- Be open to the Holy Spirit to develop the fruit of love, joy, and peace among people of God in order to create new mission opportunities.

CHAPTER 15

Retire and Rock On

Lions that retire in a zoo have it made. They are sheltered and safe, fed regularly and cared for, and viewed as noble creatures. Lions living in the jungle or wilderness have no retirement plan; each day's challenge is to hunt for food, defend your life and pride, and adapt to aging and ailments. Lions in natural settings adapt and make the best of each day, making their habitat their home and moving as needed. In either situation, lions face numerous adjustments.

Facing and preparing for retirement is a leadership challenge. I am now seventy-four. I have shared my struggles and success, wounds and wisdom, love and joy with you in the hope that my suggestions help you to the next phase in your life. We can be encouraged by what Edgar M. Bronfam and Catherine Whitney have to say in their book, *The Third Act: Reinventing Yourself After Retirement.*[24] It tells several stories of people that discovered new work and volunteer opportunities and were able to take another bow for their achievements and opportunities in later years.

> *You Approach Your Retirement*
>
> Make use of the 3-H planning approach and identify (a) your top *hopes* for your retirement years, (b) your major *hurdles* in your retirement, and (c) several ways to receive and give *help* to experience a meaningful retirement.

This chapter concerns our retirement years, which bring new challenges and opportunities. Emily Brandon reported in 2013 that a recent HSBC (founded by the Hong Kong and Shanghai Banking Corporation Limited) survey asked current employees what they hoped to do in their retirement.[25] The respondents indicated eleven hopes with the following preferences by percentages:

1. Spend more time with family and friends   59 percent
2. Travel   40 percent
3. Improve your home   36 percent
4. Keep working   34 percent
5. Volunteer   33 percent
6. Learn something new   31 percent
7. Exercise   31 percent
8. Reward yourself with a new car or other item   17 percent
9. Experience another culture   12 percent
10. Write a book   12 percent
11. Start a new business   12 percent

> *You Choose a Retirement Lifestyle*
>
> Choose all the actions from the list that appeal to you, then pick your top three priorities.

Stories of courageous retired people inspire me. As academic dean at Suomi College years ago, I pondered my morning coffee at my desk after the first snowfall in October. My secretary, Millie, escorted a new student into my office and with a Yooper (that is, a person from the Upper Peninsula of Michigan) accent, he announced, "My name is Louie, and I'm eighty-one. My girlfriend Lydia is seventy-four, and all she does is work, work, and work. So I told her we needed to celebrate and have some fun. Let's go to the polka party at the town hall on Saturday night. We did, and after a few steps, Lydia looked me in the eye and said, 'Louie, dancing with you is like dancing with a fence post.' So that's why I'm here, Dean. Where and when is the folk dance class you're offering? Lydia and I would like to enroll. We need some new steps." In that moment I discovered that you're never too old to learn, and it's never too late to start.

Carol is an excellent dancer and artist, while I am slower of foot. We look forward to enrolling in some dancing lessons. My right hip surgery in mid-August 2014 was successful, and physical therapists have me moving. This resurgence has enabled me to do part-time pastoral work at Christus Victor Lutheran Church in Elk Grove Village, Illinois.

In July 2010, before our wedding service, Carol and I agreed that we could learn some new steps for our retirement years by starting a business. We considered our prior experiences. Carol retired from her work at the Christianity Today International, which began with a publication started by Billy Graham Center and is based in Wheaton, Illinois. She enrolled in courses at Elgin Community College on personal financial management and computer graphic design. Her hands-on experience in redesigning and rehabbing her family home in Elgin resulted in a profitable sale before moving to her townhome. In my former life with Judy, we moved often to different areas, purchasing and selling various family homes. We also rehabbed the Puotinen family farmhouse and grounds before selling it for a profit. So, as newlyweds, Carol and I envisioned real-estate investing as a way to ensure future income when I retired from the pastorate.

You Supplement Your Income

Select one to three ways other than savings, Social Security, and pension plans that you can use to acquire additional funds for your goals during your retirement years.

To start, we signed up for written and video materials on real-estate investing offered by Robert Allen of *No Money Down* fame. One of his coaches called us once a week to guide us in making offers to buy a home using a subject-to approach with seller-assisted financing that culminated in a deal with another buyer. A local Elgin realtor went with us to several properties and guided our efforts. We made offers on several houses that looked promising, but the sellers wanted a cash offer, rather than a subject-to clause. As newbies, we were unaware of various options for closing the deal.

You Need a Coach

Indicate where you learned new skills and strategies when starting a new hobby, business, or self-improvement plan and how you rate the service provided by your coach.

Several months later, a webinar featuring Phill and Shenoah Grove of Austin, Texas, introduced us to Love American Homes and their REI Matcher program. It links online buyers, sellers, and investors with an automated marketing program. Data collection on a particular property details twelve different approaches to making purchase offers to motivated sellers.

Phill, a former engineer turned successful real-estate investor, specialized initially in short sales of homes in their region, and his wife, Shenoah, a licensed realtor, developed a local REI organization that has attracted experienced and new investors for information sharing and making real-estate deals together. We were attracted to their no-hype, factual, and thorough approach to real-estate investing. They came to the Chicago area for a two-day workshop that we attended, and we enjoyed meeting them.

At the Grove event, two other leaders in the real-estate field and other business ventures, JT Foxx and Raymond Aaron, hosted their own event in the same venue. Both are native Canadians with different pathways to success. JT Foxx came to Chicago with little money, began real-estate investing, and hosts his own radio show. As his fortunes improved, he pioneered the Mega Partnering event held twice a year in different cities. Major speakers in real estate, Internet marketing, and other business topics are on each program, which brings enterprising coaching students, investors, and other leaders together for networking, and making deals.

In October 2012, Carol and I attended the Mega Partnering event held in Chicago and heard former New York Mayor Rudy Giuliani speak about his leadership experience during the 9-11 terrorist attacks as well as other informative speakers. JT Foxx now owns many businesses and is an internationally recognized business coach and entrepreneur.

Two coaches from JT Foxx's organization helped us. Initially Kristyne contacted us by phone from Utah and focused our efforts in Elgin. Later Mike, who was based in Chicago, met with us personally on how to start investing in real estate, took us to see his own investment properties, and connected us with his colleagues. He introduced us to Ben, a realtor, and a contractor named John. They assisted Carol and her stepmother, Florence, in upgrading and selling Flo's townhome after she decided to relocate to an independent living center.

We continued working with Ben and two of his partners, RG and Tom, in the selling of our own home in 2014. Upon my retirement from Bethlehem Church in July 2013 we downsized our possessions and relocated to my rental property, my former home with Judy. The family that rented the property was unable to buy the home when their three-year lease concluded. We moved in during December of 2013 and January of 2014. Once you retire from a full-time position, the loss of monthly income requires numerous adjustments, including moving in the middle of winter.

You Decide to Write a Book

Suppose you desire to write a book to help other people, to advance your career, or to solve a problem. Identify a topic for one or more of these three goals that especially interests you.

My first year of retirement was not a vacation but a time for numerous household tasks, moving details, and financial matters. My opportunities to do supply preaching at several congregations in Chicagoland on Sundays kept me in touch with parish life, new friends, and my profession. This renewed parish activity led to me becoming an interim associate pastor at Christus Victor Lutheran Church in Elk Grove Village, Illinois, in October 2014, during their search for a long-term associate pastor. The congregation has a thousand members, dynamic worship experiences, and extensive outreach ministries in the community. Senior Pastor Stefan Potuznik leads a talented team of staff members and volunteers to fulfill the congregational Christian mission. I completed a ten-month term and enjoyed working with others in this caring place.

I also resumed working on this book, which was inspired by my coach Raymond Aaron, a best-selling author with several books and an international speaking career.[26] In presentations, he shares his experiences while training for and completing a twenty-six-mile race to the North Pole on foot that extended his personal limits. His most recent book is *How You Can Get Rich Without Getting Cold*. He has presented on the same platform with such figures as Bill Clinton and Richard Branson. At one conference we attended, he inspired the preparation of this book by announcing the formation of a new 10-10-10 program. Everybody can write a book, he said, using this approach. It just requires ten chapters of your own words with ten hours of your time and ten weeks to have the book printed.

At Raymond's writers' boot camp in Toronto, we met several published 10-10-10 authors and some famous writers, such as John Gray, who wrote *Men Are from Mars, Women Are from Venus*. It took me longer than 10-10-10 to write this book, and now the fruit of my creative, persistent effort is before you.

The *Lead with Courage* title inspired the formation of our new family business, known as ACLION Investments LLC. Carol and I chose the lion as a symbol for courage, leadership, and persistence, and the name is our initials, A and C, plus *LION*. These personal attributes are essential to succeed in the fields of business, education, real estate, human services, the arts, and self-development. Together our many years of significant service and success in these fields have given us experience, insights, and passion to share with friends and clients.

The mission of ACLION Investments LLC is to help people succeed and to invest in valuable properties. Our main goals are

- To assist motivated home sellers, investors, and buyers to complete beneficial real-estate transactions
- To help individuals and organizations plan, organize, and fund their programs and projects
- To offer valuable items and information to clients through publications, presentations, radio and television, and the Internet.

In our business planning, we receive assistance from the Illinois Small Business Development Center at Elgin Community College. This book profiles our leadership experiences and resources for your reading and further exploration. Carol's paintings are available for viewing and purchase. See www.artforall.com to view some of her paintings. We share our experiences and insights for your consideration as we continue building our business, and we hope to link with you in mutually beneficial growth opportunities. We like to work with people, and we welcome you to contact us at artpuotinen@att.net for further information.

You Take Another Bow

You are invited to give a presentation to a group on your life and work experiences. What are the main topics you will cover?

Suggestions for Your Ventures Together

- **Share values, an entrepreneurial spirit, and vision.** You will need to be able to communicate effectively with your partner to make decisions, set goals, and drive the business forward. If you partner with someone that is reluctant, combative, or unable to consider your viewpoint, it will be harder to be successful.

- **Bring skills and experience to your business.** A good business partner should have skills that support and complement your own. No single person is a master of all things. The more skills you and your partner bring to the business together, the easier it will be to start, plan, grow, and run your business.

- **Clearly define roles and responsibilities.** Your partner shows up to work. Now what? Don't assume the partner is on the same page as you. Make sure you each have defined roles and responsibilities that will help you understand the expected deliverables. Get it in writing, and have a business attorney prepare a partnership agreement for you.

- **Offer resources and credibility to your business.** It is great to have a business partner that has financial resources, but a partner can bring other contributions that can be just as valuable. A partner with a strong business network, industry connections, client list, or credentials and expertise can also increase the value of your business and improve your chances for achieving long-term success.

- **Practice good personal and business ethics.** Enter into partnerships only with someone you can trust. Look for someone who values honesty and practices good personal and business ethics. Use legal counsel and written contracts in your agreements to protect your business and its dealings.

- **Be financially stable.** Money, assets, and time-management skills are critical for small business entrepreneurs. Someone who has grossly mismanaged his personal or business finances may not have the skills or discipline to make a business partnership work.

- **Develop your business plan.** Work together to prepare a one- to three-year business plan. Identify major goals, desired outcomes, and action plans to achieve them. Monitor progress weekly, and make any needed modifications.

- **Respect is essential for success.** You should partner with someone that you respect and who respects you. The main purpose in forming a partnership is to achieve success as a team, so be prepared to make adjustments for individual preferences, work styles, etc.
- **Resolve together any problems.** Problems and conflicts can occur with clients, suppliers, and entities. Develop ways to deal with them effectively and to strengthen the business services you provide.

199

Afterword

You Fulfill Your Promise

Write a book that includes your struggles, setbacks and successes.

My daughter Marji wrote me the following encouragement midway through the composition of these chapters:

> Dad, I urge you to consider that the most powerful examples may be the ones you may not at first see as ending in a success or which you may think don't show you as a leader because you made mistakes. Here I'm proposing that you define success as "never giving up. That means never giving up on who you are, who you want to be, your ideals, your guiding values—instead using those to learn from mistakes and turn failure into triumph (a recurring theme of your life).
>
> Don't leave out examples where you made mistakes—instead show how you learned from them and adapted accordingly. The stories that show where you struggled the most and made the most mistakes, yet still persisted, are the most powerful ones. But that is OK—because a challenge really represents the opportunity to feel the satisfaction of

overcoming it. The greater and more painful the challenge, the sweeter is the reward.

Marji expresses an approach to life that is passed on from one generation to another in the Puotinen family. The Finns have a word for it: *sisu*. A person with sisu is a person of substance—not a sissy—who is known for courage, endurance, strength, and persistence. My grandparents and parents shared this legacy with their family, friends, and community. A great lion named Winston Churchill said, "Success is not final, failure is not fatal: it is the courage to continue that counts."

Whatever your situation is today, remember God loves you and unleashes your strength and courage to be the person you are called to be. Christians like to *roarr* about our baptism and remember it as our pool of discovery of who and whose we are. At the baptismal font or pool, we receive the promises of the Lord Jesus Christ in the water and Word of our baptism. Sprinkled with or immersed in water, each infant or adult receives the refreshing Word. We are cleansed of sin, joined to the family of God, promised eternal life, and given spiritual gifts of faith and other blessings.

God the Creator is with you. Christ lives in you. The Spirit moves and empowers you. Now unleash the lion in you, and lead with courage so that others may hear your strong voice, see your good work, and glorify God throughout your life journey.

Endnotes

1   See "Symbolic Meaning of Lions," what's your sign.com.

2   The primary source for lion information in most chapter beginnings is from Christine and Michel Deniis-Huot, *The Art of Being a Lion* (New York: Friedman/Fairfax Publishers, 2002).

3   See the following publications by Arthur E. Puotinen:

"Copper Country Clergy Quest: Pastoral Action in Labor Relations," *Lutheran Forum*, August/September 1971.

"Ameliorative Factors in the Conflict between the Suomi Synod and Socialism," in *Faith of the Finns: Historical Perspectives in Finnish Lutheranism in America*, ed. Ralph J. Jalkanen (Lansing: Michigan State University Press, 1972), pp. 227-249.

"Copper Country Finns and the Strike of 1913," in *The Finnish Experience in the Western Great Lakes Region: New Perspectives*, eds. Michael Karni et al. (Turku, Finland: Institute for Migration, 1975), pp. 143-153

"Early Labor Organizations in the Copper Country," in *For the Common Good*, eds. Michael G. Karni and Douglas J. Ollila Jr. (Superior, WI: Tyomies Publishing Company, 1977), pp. 119-166.

Arthur Edwin Puotinen, *Finnish Radicals and Religion in Midwestern Mining Towns, 1865-1914* (New York: Arno Press, 1979).

"Church and Labor Conflict in Northern Michigan," in *Finnish Diaspora in United States*, ed. Michael G. Karni (Toronto: The Multicultural-History Society of Ontario, 1981).

This excerpt of an overview of the "Finnish Folklore and Social Change in the Great Lake Mining Region" Oral History Project for Suomi College and partially funded by the National Endowment for Humanities is noted in the Finnish American Historical Archives link of Finlandia University, www.finlandia.edu/oral-history-project.

A partial summary of the research design developed in 1972 by Dr. Arthur Puotinen includes the following:

> Research problem: How have the local people in the Lake Superior mining region coped with the decline of a major copper and iron mining industry and its detrimental effects? What resources have they developed to meet the challenge?

> Nature of the project: Beginning in the summer of 1972, this formative or explorative study will seek insights from persons generally sixty-five years and older that have personally lived through this transition phase. The oral history interview will focus on primarily two objectives:

> 1. To seek basic information from all participants and
> 2. To encourage spontaneous recollections from persons regarding areas of special interest in their life and experiences.

> These interviews will be secured from Finnish Americans and persons from other ethnic groups as well.

> Suggested areas for questioning:

> a) Personal history—five questions
> b) Education—seven questions
> c) Employment—seven questions
> d) Politics—six questions
> e) Social life—ten questions
> f) Medicine—eight questions
> g) Religion—six questions

Interviewers adapted these questions to focus on individual backgrounds of their volunteer. Interviews occurred in various locales, generally lasted an hour or so and were tape-recorded. Audiotapes were sent to the project director, Arthur Puotinen, and transcribed by Esther Pekkala for cataloging in the Finnish American Historical Archives.

5   Sara Puotinen and her husband, Scott Anderson, filmed two videos of the Puotinen family farm and Puotinen family women that are available on their website: www.room34.com.

6   Outward Bound US was founded fifty years ago by Kurt Hahn. It is the leading experiential education program in the United States, with a network of regional schools across the country. It exists to "weave the thread of character, leadership and ethic of service into the fabric of the local community." The Lenoir-Rhyne College teams enjoyed their nine-day experiences at either Blue Ridge Mountain School or the Asheville School. My experiences were at the Asheville School.

7   Lutheran Film Associates contracted with film directors Bill Jersey and Barbara Connell to film unscripted events. They happened as people expressed themselves. The directors edited extensive film footage and produced the final version. *A Time for Burning*, released in 1966 and still available, received a nomination for the Academy Award for Best Documentary Film.

8   Clergy and Laymen Concerned About Vietnam (CALCAV) was officially founded on October 28, 1965, at the Church Center for the United Nations by Rev. Richard Neuhaus (Lutheran pastor), Rabbi Abraham Joshua Heschel (Jewish scholar and professor), and Fr. Daniel Berrigan SJ (prominent Catholic voice against the war).

Martin Luther King Jr. became national cochair, strengthening the breadth and reach of this new national organization. Neither pacifist nor radical, CALCAV was seen as a moderate movement, drawing upon the biblical roots of peacemaking as well as the strong tradition of democratic dissent. It was a highly influential religious voice for ending the war. After the war ended, it changed its name to Clergy and Laity Concerned (CALC) and worked on a number of national and international peace and justice issues.

9   See William Manchester and Paul Reid, *The Last Lion: Winston Spencer Churchill* (Little, Brown and Company, 2012). Regarding the importance of the Lion symbol in Finland, see Coat of arms of Finland - Wikipedia. org. For more information regarding Lions Club international, see www. lionsclubs.org. Founded on June 7, 1917, by Melvin Jones, this secular service club is headquartered in Oak Brook, Illinois, and has 1.35 million members. Its motto is "We Serve."

10 As LECNA executive director, I edited the published annual meeting presentations, reports, and other information for 1984–88. This chapter refers to events and experiences referred to in *Seventy-five Years of LECNA: the Pursuit of Opportunity: Papers and Proceedings of the 75th Anniversary Meeting, Lutheran Educational Conference of North America, LECNA, 1985.* Also see *Increasing International Dimensions of Lutheran Higher Education: Papers and Proceedings of the 75th Anniversary Meeting, Lutheran Educational Conference of North America, LECNA, 1988.*

11 Several LECNA Program Grants were awarded by Lutheran Brotherhood and Aid Association of Lutherans. Lutheran Brotherhood was founded in 1917 as Lutheran Union and in 1920 changed its name to Lutheran Brotherhood. Similarly, Aid Association of Lutherans was founded in 1902 and provided its members financial services and products. The AAL and LB functioned independently throughout the twentieth century. In June 2001, after close consideration of how combining the two organizations would be of benefit to members, the AAL and LB merged, with the merger completed by the end of that year. In 2002 a new name was approved by the members of the merged organization: Thrivent Financial for Lutherans. In June 2013, members voted to allow non-Lutheran Christians to join, and in March 2014 the marketing name was shortened to Thrivent Financial.

12 Huot, *The Art of Being a Lion*, pp. 132–33.

13 The City of Des Moines has fifty-eight organized neighborhood associations, with Union Park Neighborhood Association being one of them. UPNA started with a group of people including Margaret Swanson, Fred Gay, Bill Ritchie, Bill Horstman, and Harold McMurray. They met frequently to determine boundaries, elect officers, write bylaws, and finally make an application to the city. In 1991, UPNA became a designated neighborhood, and community input went into an action plan that was developed. In 1993, the plan was approved, and it became a recognized neighborhood.

14   Herbert Chilstrom, *A Journey of Grace: The Formation of a Leader and a Church* (Minneapolis: Huff Publishing Associates, Lutheran University Press, 2011), p. 402.

15   The *Des Moines Register* was founded in 1849 as the *Iowa Star*. It is now owned by Gannett Company and located in Des Moines. The newspaper has a circulation of nearly ninety-eight thousand daily readers and over two hundred thousand Sunday readers. The November 19, 1988, issue carried the first report of the rape incident on the Grand View campus.

16   The mastermind principle and practices are detailed by Napoleon Hill in "Power of the Master Mind," *Think and Grow Rich* (New York: Penguin, 2007), pp. 139–45, and in "Master Mind," *The Magic Ladder to Success* (New York: Penguin), pp. 217–56.

17   Rudolph W. Giuliani, *Leadership* (New York: Hyperion Press), 2002. See chapter 1, "September 11, 2001," for the mayor's dramatic portrayal of September 11 events and chapter 16, "Recovery," for his assessment of progress. The JT Foxx Mega Partnering event at Oak Brook, Illinois, featured the keynote presentation by Mayor Giuliani on October 28, 2011. The quotations are from my notes of his speech that day.

18   Patricia Ripley, "Remembering the Flood of 1993," DSM H20 Des Moines Water Works Blog, July 10, 2013.

19   The following report is based on documents I wrote during the financial recovery period and shared with constituents.

20   Thorvald Hansen, *That All Good Seed Strike Root: A Centennial History of Grand View College* (Des Moines, Iowa: Grand View College, 1996).

21   Armas J. Holmio, trans. Ellen Ryynanen, *History of the Finns in Michigan* (Detroit: Wayne State University Press, 2001), pp.393–404, provides a brief history of both Suomi Seminary and Suomi

See Arnold Stadius, "Suomi College and Seminary," in *Finns in North America: A Social Symposium*, ed. Ralph J. Jalkanen (East Lansing, MI: Michigan State University Press, 1969).

See also Ralph J. Jalkanen, ed., *The Faith of the Finns* (Michigan State University Press, 1972), provides chapters by Douglas J Ollila Jr. (pp. 158–75) and Olaf Rankinen (pp. 176–94) that relate to the histories of both educational institutions.

22   The Jutila Center for Global Design and Business is described in the Finlandia University.edu web page.

[23] Sara Puotinen, "Living and Grieving Beside Judith," *Mothering, Bereavement, Loss and Grief, Journal of the Motherhood Initiative for Research and Community Involvement* 1, no. 2 (Fall/Winter 2010): p. 97.

[24] Edgar M. Bronfam and Catherine Whitney, *The Third Act: Reinventing Yourself After Retirement* (New York: Putnam Adult, 2002).

[25] Emily Brandon, "Ten Things to Do in Retirement," *U.S. News and World Report*, March 1, 2013.

[26] Raymond Aaron is a *New York Times* best-selling author, leading success and investment coach, and syndicated radio personality. He is the author of *Chicken Soup for the Parent's Soul, Chicken Soup for the Canadian Soul,* and *Double Your Income Doing What You Love.*